GRAND BIKEPACKING JOURNEYS

Riding Iconic Routes around the World

gestalten

CONTENTS

FOREWORD

4 *Recreational Nomadism*

JOURNEYS

10 *Tuscany Trail*
22 *Torino-Nice Rally*
32 *Raid Pyrénées*
40 *Tour du Mont Blanc*
50 *GR247*
60 *GranGuanche*
70 *Adriatic Crest*
84 *Transcaucasian Trail*
94 *Cairngorms Loop*
106 *Iceland Divide*
122 *Oregon Timber Trail*
130 *Colorado Trail*
138 *Great Divide Mountain Bike Route*
150 *Iditarod Trail*
162 *Peru Divide*
178 *La Ruta Mala*
190 *The Cross Cape*
202 *Bartang Valley and Pamir Highway*
212 *The Middle Lands*
224 *Annapurna Circuit*
236 *Ha Giang Loop*
250 *Tour Aotearoa*
262 *The Hunt 1000*

HOW TOS

6 *Bikes, Bags, & Setups*
8 *Master Kit Grid*
104 *Shelter*
120 *Trailside Fixes*
148 *Coping With Extremes*
188 *Traveling in Groups*
222 *Traveling in Remote Environments*
248 *Getting to and from Your Route*

APPENDIX

270 *Index*
272 *Imprint*

RECREATIONAL NOMADISM

FOREWORD
STEFAN AMATO

"See?" said one of our group, as we rode among galloping herds on the Son-Kul plain in Kyrgyzstan, "All you really need in life is a horse or a bicycle." I thought about this for the remainder of our bikepack through the Tian Shan Mountains, and once the double-track dust had settled, realized that nomadism intrigues, fulfills, and connects no more so than over a shared track or cups of warming chai. Life under yurt-dotted, snowcapped horizons was simple—simple, but tough—largely born out of heritage or necessity, rather than choice. Yet, for one week, we'd chosen to be nomads too, carrying everything we needed for a week in the wilds on our all-road bicycles. We were recreational nomads seeking escape and adventure with bikes as steeds, tents as shelter, plov as sustenance, and routes as reason.

Penned across two different trips, in Kyrgyzstan and Scotland, the lands that these pages describe sum up bikepacking for me: a healthy mix of bucket-list trips, discovering faraway lands and cultures, and opportunistic weekend escapes close to home—all equally valid. The classic and future-classic bikepacking routes, photography, and words over the following pages celebrate where a bike can take you. Tried and tested, these routes offer adventure templates and inspiration for our growing community of recreational nomads, from a lengthy, high-altitude, off-road trip through Peru, to a 200-kilometer (124-mile) loop of the Cairngorms National Park, where I'm currently sitting, just outside Ryvoan Bothy, writing this introduction. I use the word "templates" because that is what these routes are—follow them to the meter, shorten, or section them to suit your timeframe or riding style, extend them further to intensify the adventure, connect with additional routes and cities, or simply use them as a spark to plot your own bikepacking adventures.

The term "bikepacking" hosts a number of camps now, from roamers, to route-makers and racers. The last time I was at Son-Kul, I was racing the 1,700-kilometer (1,056-mile) Silk Road Mountain Race as sleet fell through sunny yet stormy skies. We rushed into the checkpoint yurt for some warming plov and chai before riding onwards, motivated to reach the next checkpoint some 400 kilometers (250 miles) away. This time, we swam in the lake's glacial waters, marveled at intensely starry skies, watched real nomads at work, rode bikes with kids, and sipped our chai. There are any number of ways of exploring by bike. The only way of knowing what suits you is to get out there—you might surprise yourself, and your boundaries. For example, racer-minded bikepackers might notice the term "ITT" in this book, meaning Individual Time Trial. These are increasingly popular timed records along classic bikepacking routes, up for grabs whenever you want to try riding fast. The rules? You must be 100 percent self-supported and record/submit your route/time digitally for verification. Otherwise, slowly does it; slow is OK too.

Going forward, bikepacking has an important role to play in the need for ecologically responsible tourism. Overlanding and human-powered nomadism by bike really is the best way of traveling—slow enough to really experience place, landscape, and culture; fast enough to cover some ground. It seems the greatest chasm is the contrast between the bike as a tool for sustainable travel, and the methods of traveling to and from the following classic routes. Races and events are slowly encouraging overland travel, but at the end of the day, it's up to you. Currently, I feel the offsetting and supporting of local communities, once on the bike, justifies the travel now and again. A lot of classic bikepacking routes are lifelines for rural communities, and the newer ones are quickly establishing themselves as such. Popular routes, such as the Great Divide, even establish their own infrastructures. However, reluctance comes with the sanitization (tarmacking) of classic routes, such as the Carretera Austral in Chile, to cater to other traffic. Intrepid bikepackers will always seek and promote the roads less traveled—it is generally where the adventure lies—despite the fact it batters bikes and bodies, minds and equipment at a much faster rate. What will a classic bikepacking-route book look like in 25, 100, or 500 years? One thing is for sure: all you really need is a bicycle. Here's to the next generation of recreational nomads…

BIKES, BAGS, & SETUPS

Ride. Drink. Eat. Sleep. Repeat. For wilderness wanderers, the development of rackless bags, lightweight technical kit, and "all-terrain" bikes mean that all the gear you need can be carried nimbly. Bike and setup versatility—the ability to both pedal off-road passes and comfortably cruise paved roads—is key for bikepacking trips. Adapt your plans to the bike and kit you have.

BIKEPACKING BAGS

Total capacity will be based on bike size and space available. Always measure and check with bag manufacturers.

1 *Seat pack (8–16 L)*
2 *Handlebar pack (8–18 L)*
3 *Handlebar pouch pack (1–3 L)*
4 *Frame pack (2–9 L)*
5 *Fork pack × 2 (6–8 L)*
6 *Top tube packs × 2 (0.5–1 L)*
7 *Down tube pack (1–2 L)*
8 *Stem packs × 2 (1–2 L)*
9 *Hip pack (2–6 L)*
= 37 L–76 L

BIKE & SETUP

Several factors have to be considered. Things like bigger tires and lower gearing are essential for heading off-road.

A *Frame material/geometry/specs*
B *Gearing/drivetrain/shifting*
C *Brakes*
D *Wheel and tire size/tread*
E *Handlebars and hand positions*
F *Mounts for racks/cages*
G *Saddle*
H *Navigation/devices*
J *Dynamo hub lighting/charging*
K *Pedals*
L *Mudguards*

BIKEPACKER

BIKE: "All-terrain" gravel, or mountain
LUGGAGE: Bikepacking bags
TRIPS AND TERRAIN: Roam anywhere. With bigger tires and a nimbler setup, carry everything you need for a few days and reach higher, more remote, and wilder worlds, even if pushing your bike is required. Space can be limited, especially for clunkier items like one-liter, or more, cooking pots and water and food supplies beyond 3–4 days. Tape your frame where bags attach and might rub.

FASTPACKER

BIKE: Road, gravel, or mountain
LUGGAGE: Bikepacking bags
TRIPS AND TERRAIN: Fast and light road and off-road adventures carrying the bare minimum. Typically shorter trips in known weathers, using accommodations. Camping and cooking are seen more as secondary, with only room for a bivvy setup, lightweight stove set, and minimal supplies.

TRADITIONAL TOURER

BIKE: Touring/expedition
LUGGAGE: Traditional pannier bags
TRIPS AND TERRAIN: Road and light off-road adventures, for as long as you want to be away. A full set of panniers not only offers more space to carry whatever you need, but is less fussy to pack and easier to take on and off the bike. However, additional weight does make the bike less agile across technical off-road terrain—the reason for the development of "rackless" bikepacking bags.

ALTERNATIVES

BIKE: Various
LUGGAGE: Trailers, racks, baskets, backpacks
TRIPS AND TERRAIN: Various. Mix things up! A bikepacker setup with the addition of front panniers or a backpack can carry enough supplies and equipment for a few more days in the wild, and does not affect technical off-road capabilities too much. For adventures with kids, add a trailer to a "fastpacker" setup.

21
23
22
27
33
36
42
38
37
39
40
41
49
20
19
52
51
50
48
46
45
47
54
53
55
43
6
11
7
8
44
1
2
5

MASTER KIT GRID

Self-sufficiency in the world's wilds means each trip calls for a different kit list. Here are the basics to consider:

RIDING CLOTHING

1 *Helmet/cap*
2 *Sunglasses*
3 *Rugged shoes (SPD/flats)*
4 *Socks*
5 *Padded bib shorts*
6 *Over-shorts*
7 *Base layer*
8 *Shirt/jersey*
9 *Wind/waterproof jacket*
10 *Insulated layer*
11 *Wind/waterproof pants*
12 *Mitts/gloves*
13 *Buff*

OFF-THE-BIKE CLOTHING

14 *Cozy insulated jacket*
15 *Shirt*
16 *Leggings*
17 *Underwear*
18 *Warm hat*
19 *Warm socks*
20 *Shoes/sandals*

SHELTER

21 *Tent*
22 *Sleeping mat/pillow*
23 *Sleeping bag/quilt*

COOKING, WATER, DRINKS, & FOOD

24 *Stove*
25 *Fuel/lighter*
26 *Pot(s)*
27 *Spork/knife*
28 *Mug*
29 *Coffee/tea equipment*
30 *Water filter*
31 *Water bottles/bladder*
32 *Insulated/hip flasks*
33 *Snacks*
34 *Food supplies*
35 *Drink supplies*
36 *Trash bags*

WASHBAG

37 *Toothbrush/toothpaste*
38 *Travel towel*
39 *Tissues/biodegradable wet wipes*
40 *Sunscreen*
41 *Bug/bear spray*
42 *Toilet trowel*

FIRST AID KIT

43 *See "Trail-side Fixes" p. 120*

TOOLS & SPARES

44 *See "Trail-side Fixes" p. 120*

ELECTRONICS

45 *GPS device*
46 *Smartphone*
47 *Camera*
48 *Front and rear lights*
49 *Headlamp*
50 *USB battery pack/spare batteries*
51 *Wall charger/charging cables*
52 *Headphones*

MISCELLANEOUS

53 *Map/compass*
54 *Sketchbook/pen*
55 *Wallet/passport/insurance*
56 *Cable lock*

RIDING UNDER THE TUSCAN SUN

ROUTE:
TUSCANY TRAIL

LOCATION:
ITALY

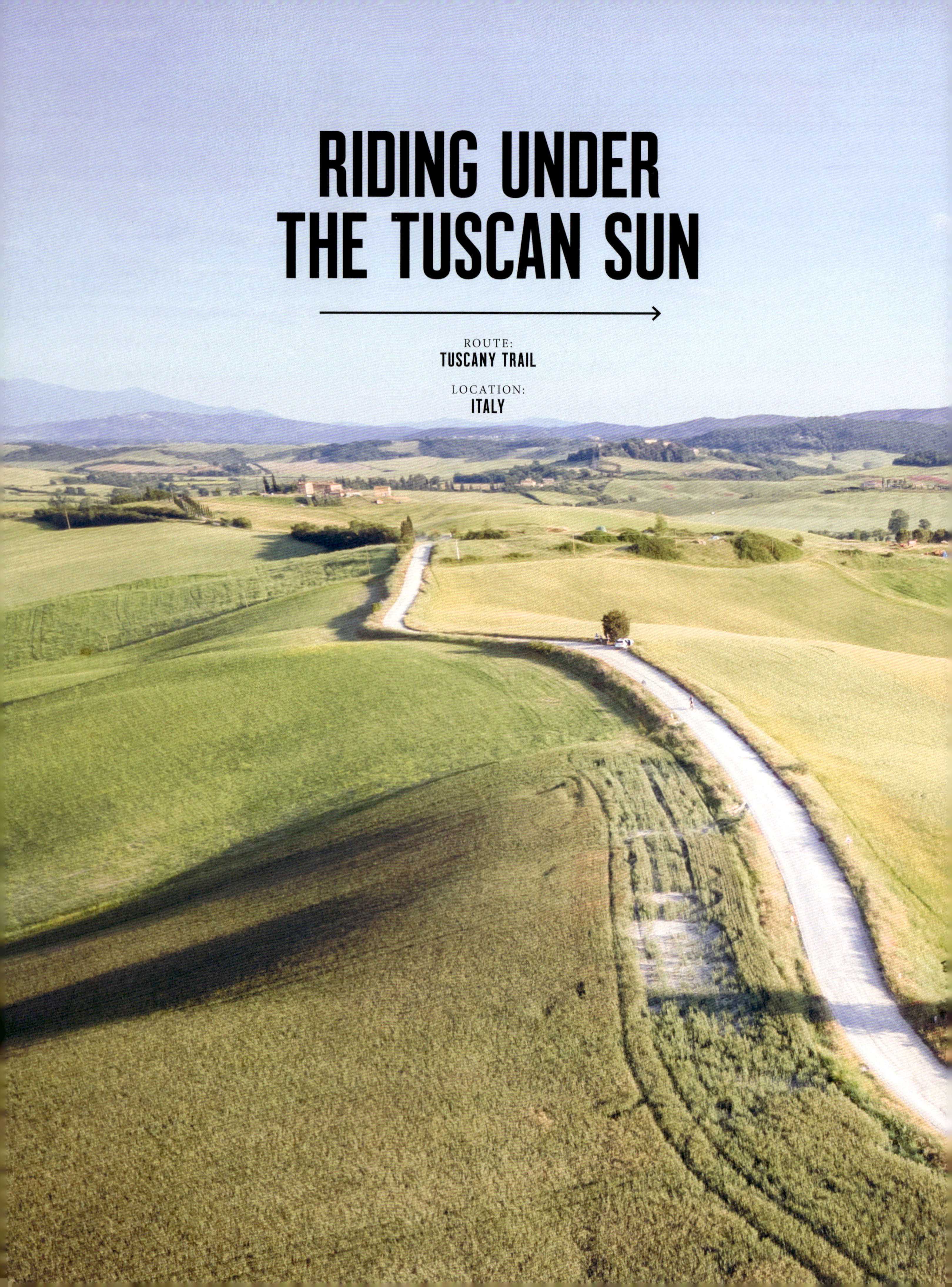

THE TRAIL LINKS TOGETHER TUSCANY'S STUNNING MEDIEVAL AND RENAISSANCE TOWNS AND HILLTOP VILLAGES.

FORGET ENERGY GELS AND BARS, TUSCANY'S FINEST FOOD AND WINE IS NEVER TOO FAR AWAY—"CUCINA POVERA" IS OFTEN IDEAL BIKEPACKING CUISINE.

SOME AREAS OF THE GLOBAL CYCLING community—especially those of a road bike persuasion—worship at the altar of the Latin phrase, "ex duris gloria." To them, there is glory in suffering, or, more accurately: "From suffering comes glory."

The Tuscany Trail starts just down the road from Rome, the birthplace of the Latin language, but the idea that this ride should be a suffer-fest is anathema to the likes of route organizer Andrea Borchi. On the Tuscany Trail, you're never more than a few miles' ride from a pasticceria or a perfect cappuccino (only before 11:00 a.m. remember—drinking milky coffee in the afternoon is severely frowned upon in Italy). To Andrea, riding and experiencing all the trail has to offer is as much about the time spent in Tuscan trattorias as it is on two wheels.

This description is certainly not to downplay the banana-shaped route from top to bottom, north to south, of the region. Or, indeed, the fitness required to complete a 470-kilometer (292-mile) ride, much of which is on dirt roads and gravel. But with "only" →

TUSCANY'S ROLLING HILLS, STRADE BIANCHE, AND CLIMATE MAKE FOR AN IDEAL BIKEPACKING PLAYGROUND.

"I ABSORBED A NEW SENSE OF TIME—SLOWER HERE, LESS URGENT."

IN TERMS OF OFF-ROAD RIDING, TUSCANY'S TERRAIN AND RESUPPLY OPTIONS PROVIDE A GREAT INTRODUCTION TO BIKEPACKING.

7,000 meters (22,966 feet) of climbing across the ride, it has a mellower feel, and certainly a more mellow vibe, summed up by Andrea's attitude to refueling. The idea of digging out your camp stove and boiling water for a re-hydrated meal? Borderline offensive. "We don't cook along the Tuscany Trail, we sit at the table to eat in the restaurants, tavernas, cafes along the way," he says.

And if being stocked up on laminated dough snacks and caffeine isn't enough, you're also overloaded with an incredible landscape to ride through, a feast for all the senses. The glory of the Tuscany Trail is in its incredible beauty. The limestone gravel white roads—strade bianche—that cut through vineyards and olive groves in the Tuscan countryside have been described as nature's gift to cycling. The American author Frances Mayes went further in her iconic book about the region, *Under the Tuscan Sun*. "My idea of heaven still is to drive the gravel farm roads of Umbria and Tuscany, very pleasantly lost."

Finding your way on the Tuscany Trail should be easy enough though. The route was devised by Andrea for an annual bikepacking event, reportedly the largest of its kind on the planet (3,000 people rode the event in May 2022) and there is a GPX file available to download.

The route has been refined and rejigged down the years and the 2022 iteration begins in the medieval seaside village of Castagneto Carducci, 80 kilometers (50 miles) south of Pisa. Appropriately, given the beauty of the route, the start village is named after a former winner of the Nobel Prize for literature, Giosuè Carducci. The route finishes at the ocean in Orbetello. As the crow flies, the start and finish towns are 100 kilometers (62 miles) apart but this ride is not about getting from A to B in the fastest possible time. It's about an experience—absorbing and consuming, everything that riding under the Tuscan sun offers—and channeling a little bit of your inner Mayes on the way. As the American author said of living in the region: "I absorbed a new sense of time—slower here, less urgent." The only urgency really is to get a trip booked to ride this route. As the Italians would say, *andiamo*. Let's go. ○

TUSCANY PROVIDES THE OPPORTUNITY FOR ESCAPE AND SOLITUDE BEYOND THE BUSTLING CITY CENTERS—A HEALTHY MIX OF MILD AND WILD.

ROUTE NOTES

Start: Castagneto Carducci, Italy / **Finish:** Orbetello, Italy / **Distance:** 470 km (292 mi) / **Duration:** 5–7 days / **Category:** Multiday point-to-point / **Terrain:** 65 % off-road / **Level:** Easy-Moderate

LOCAL SPECIALTIES:

As the Tuscany Trail website says: "Forget the energy bars." Finding food is not a problem; you're rarely more than a few miles away from civilization on the trail. Knowing when to stop could be more of an issue given the incredible cuisine the region offers. It's generally inspired by humble peasant food that uses a handful of ingredients, such as ribollita—a Tuscan bean soup made with cannellini beans, bread, and vegetables.

WILDLIFE AND LANDSCAPE:

The landscape is as beautiful as it is varied. One minute the route is heading through the iconic rolling green hills of the Val d'Orcia, the next you are in the medieval city of Siena, a UNESCO World Heritage Site, before finishing on the coast.

RESUPPLY NOTES:

No big issues here with cafes and trattorias aplenty. In the height of summer, the temperature is regularly above 30 °C (86 °F), so having enough water is definitely something to keep an eye on.

ACCOMMODATIONS:

Tuscany is not only a bikepacker's paradise—it's a tourist one too. As a result, there's a wealth of accommodation options, often close to the route.

GETTING THERE (AND BACK):

There are airports (Pisa, Florence, Rome) aplenty near the start and finish. The start in Castagneto Carducci is 200 m (656 ft) from the train station, from which you can be in Pisa in under an hour.

RIDE SEASON AND CLIMATE:

Borchi organizes the Tuscany Trail event in late May/early June for a reason—days are long, temperatures are temperate, and there is very little rain. In general though, the window to ride the route is large—from spring (March) into late fall (November). In high summer, it can get very hot and dry.

EQUIPMENT:

Nothing beyond the ordinary bikepacking equipment here—spare tubes and a large water-carrying capacity should cover it.

WHAT TO RIDE:

Again, nothing groundbreaking here. Two-thirds of the route is on gravel roads, so a road bike with skinny tires is not your friend. Gravel or mountain bikes are.

ROUTEMAKER:

The route was originally designed in 2014 by the founder of the Tuscany Trail, Andrea Borchi.

CONTRIBUTOR INFO:

Andrea Borchi has been bikepacking since 2008. Why the Tuscany Trail? "It arose out of my desire to share my philosophy on the sport. It's not a race, it's an adventure."

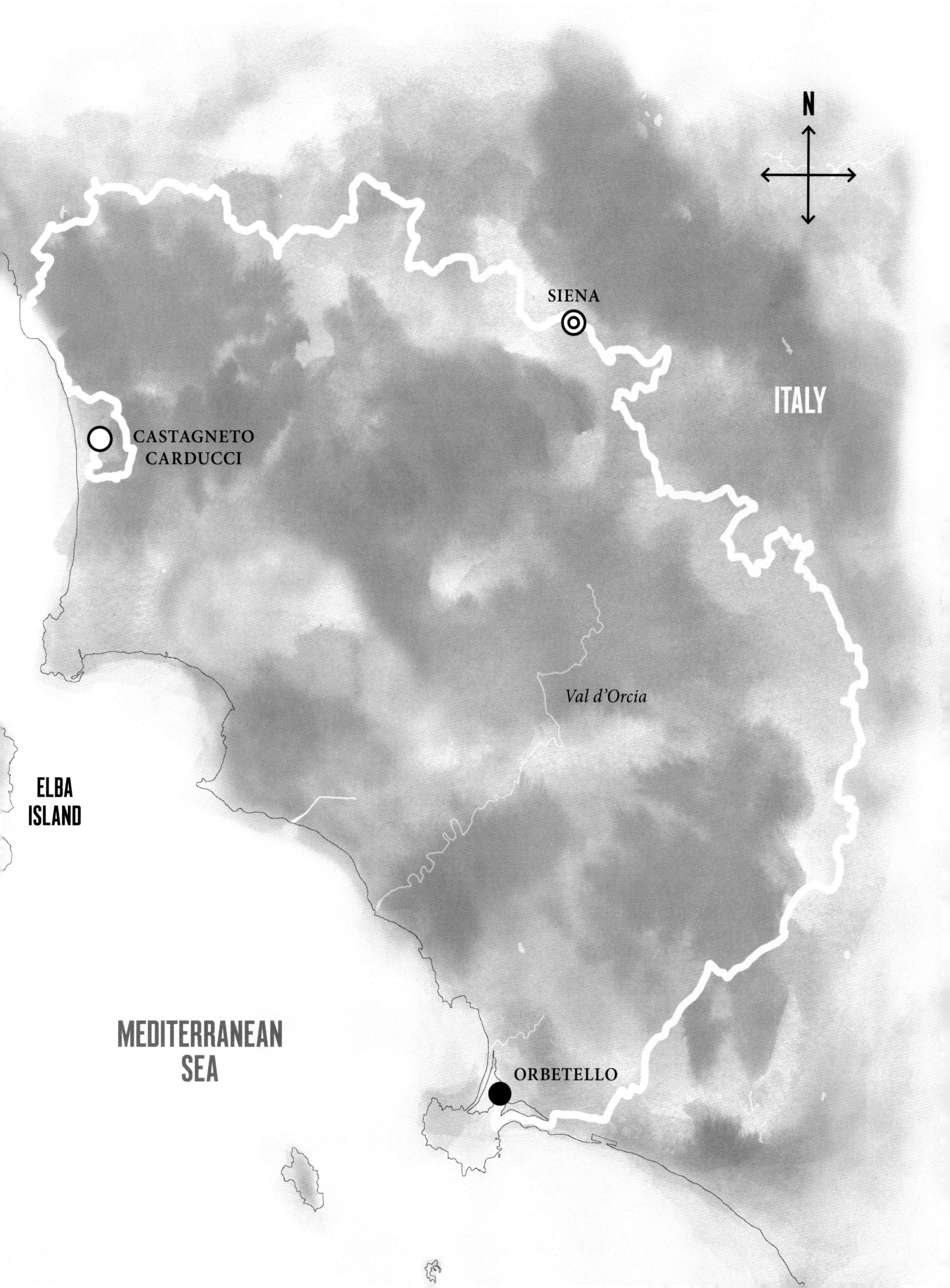
N
SIENA
ITALY
CASTAGNETO
CARDUCCI
Val d’Orcia
ELBA
ISLAND
MEDITERRANEAN
SEA
ORBETELLO

RIDE HIGH ALPINE STRADAS TO THE SEA

ROUTE:
TORINO-NICE RALLY

LOCATION:
ITALY AND FRANCE

JAMES OLSEN IS A MAN WHO LOVES researching almost as much as he loves riding. The Torino-Nice Rally was born out of his passion for both. A self-confessed fan of wide-open gravel tracks that allow time and space to take in the view, he thought the old gravel military roads that crisscross the Alps could be linked together into a spectacular route. If nothing else, it was a good excuse to pore over maps and research old books like Fred Wright's original 2002 *Rough Stuff Cycling in the Alps*, a photocopied and self-published gold mine of route ideas (for anyone prepared to hike with their bike). Immersed in the history of the Alps, Olsen roughed out the route that became the Torino-Nice Rally by dropping pins on Google Earth at the start and end points of the dramatic high dirt roads he discovered or the centers of places that looked worth exploring. Even in its skeletal form, the route included iconic road

BIG MOUNTAIN HORIZONS LINE THE WHOLE JOURNEY THROUGH THE COTTIAN AND MARITIME ALPS.

cols made famous by the Giro D'Italia and Tour de France as well as the glorious potential of endless gravel that would allow him to maintain his height in the mountains that bit longer, rather than plummeting straight down the other side.

Route planning is wonderful armchair travel, but there's often a wide gap between what we think or hope we are creating and the ride experience itself. And so Olsen took the leap and decided to find out whether his virtual line across the map would fulfill its potential. He set out with a couple of friends to ride the route in 2015 and in doing so, discovered a route that delivered even more than it promised. →

TORINO-NICE KNITS TOGETHER A MIX OF CHALLENGING GRAVEL STRADAS AND PAVED CLASSIC PASSES, LIKE THE COL AGNEL HIGH ON THE BORDER BETWEEN ITALY AND FRANCE.

Alpine switchback perfection was framed by distant peaks, mountain refuges provided shelter in the most remote of locations, and the gravel roads were of varying quality—but in the best kind of way. They tested the limits of their bikes, and occasionally forced them into pushing, but delivered views and experiences the riders never would have had if they'd stuck to the safety of tarmac.

In fact, the route was so good that Olsen decided to share it with others and organized a group start ride in 2016. Unlike many bikepacking events, Torino-Nice was to be in the tradition of motor rallies rather than a race. Those lining up weren't timed and could approach the ride however they liked. Learning from his experience the year before, Olsen tweaked the route and even provided detour options and short cuts. Ultimately, it was for each rider to set their own schedule, whether that was pushing hard all the way to a well-earned dip in the Mediterranean or ending each day early in the quest for pizza and red wine. Friendships were forged on the trail as groups naturally formed. Riders covered in the white dust of the unpaved roads sipped espressos in empty Italian village squares. Bike lights shone high up cols long after the sun had set. And over the course of about a week, more and more sets of wheels were dipped into the sea off the Promenade des Anglais in Nice.

The ethos of the event has proved hugely popular, and today, the Torino-Nice Rally (TNR) entry list rapidly fills up each year. In 2021, inspired by that welcoming atmosphere, ultra-endurance racer Lael Wilcox ran a Women's Torino-Nice Rally using Olsen's route and the TNR's rigorously casual approach to rules. It was the first bikepacking challenge exclusively for women in Europe, with a mission to demonstrate that bikepacking and ultra-distance riding is for everyone. Forty-one women took part, and each had their own adventure on the way to Nice.

And that is what makes Torino-Nice and bikepacking in general so special. Whether in a group or solo, the route is just the beginning; the true adventure occurs along the way. ○

ALPINE THEATRES LIKE THE GARDETTA PLATEAU MAKE THE CHALLENGING RIDE WORTH IT—ROUTEMAKER, JAMES, CALLS IT "LITTLE PERU."

ROUTE NOTES

Start: Turin/Torino, Italy / **Finish:** Nice, France / **Distance:** Approximately 700 km (435 mi); multiple route options are available / **Duration:** 5–10 days / **Category:** Adventurous gravel / **Terrain:** 65 % road, 35 % gravel (some quite rough) / **Level:** Moderate, with a lot of climbing

HIGHLIGHTS:

Each col has its own personality and topping out reveals a new view, opening out across the Southern Alps.

LOCAL SPECIALTIES:

It would be rude not to stop at a village bakery for a morning pastry, and keep your eyes peeled for small trattorias/pizzerias later on in the day.

WILDLIFE AND LANDSCAPE:

Enjoy the very best vistas that the Southern Alps have to offer. There's little more humbling than climbing to the crest of a 3,000 m (10,000 ft) col and seeing peaks high above you still.

RESUPPLY NOTES:

The route goes through towns and villages the entire way. Be prepared for "unusual" (read frankly unhelpful) opening times, especially on Sundays. If cafes and restaurants aren't open, the larger towns you pass through will often have a grocer or small supermarket.

ACCOMMODATIONS:

It is entirely possible to complete the ride without camping, although a lightweight camping setup will afford you more flexibility. There are many refuges/rifugios (depending on which side of the border you are) along the route, as well as hotels and Airbnb options in towns.

GETTING THERE (AND BACK):

Both Turin and Nice have airports a few kilometers out of town and near the start/finish of the route. The Torino-Nice Rally website includes a GPX riding option to/from the airports. Again, both cities are well served by a mainline train station.

RIDE SEASON:

Some of the passes are closed due to snow into early June. The weather is most stable from late June to mid-September. Valleys have the potential to be stiflingly hot in mid-summer. Be prepared for temperatures to drop high up on col sides, regardless of the time of year, and afternoon storms are always a potential threat. Mid-September is possibly the best time to ride, taking advantage of slightly lower daytime temperatures, but hopefully beating the onset of fall.

EQUIPMENT:

No specialist equipment is required. Bring clothing to cope with extremes of weather, even in the middle of summer. The route includes 20,000 m (65,617 ft) of climbing, so you'll appreciate a lighter-weight setup on the climbs.

WHAT TO RIDE:

A gravel bike is perfect for the route if you want to experience it as it was intended. However, a lightweight mountain bike might be a little more comfortable, at the price of some speed on the road sections. Tire width is a trade-off between the long tarmac miles and the off-road segments. On the whole, you are likely to enjoy the route more if you lean toward a setup that will take the off-road in its stride. Route creator James Olsen suggests a gravel bike with a high-volume 650b (27.5-in) tire as the perfect compromise.

OTHER IMPORTANT INFORMATION:

Heavy storms in the Roya Valley in 2020 have meant that some sections of the original route have now been rerouted. Make sure you use an up-to-date GPX file that takes this into account.

ROUTEMAKER:

James Olsen devised the route in 2015.

CONTRIBUTOR INFO:

Tom Gibbs is a gravel, bikepacking and adventure cyclist based in East London, U.K.

N
TORINO
Cottian Alps
FRANCE
ITALY
Maritime Alps
Roya Valley
NICE
LIGURIAN SEA

A TOUR THROUGH THE HEART OF CYCLING HISTORY

ROUTE:
RAID PYRÉNÉES

LOCATION:
FRANCE

IT WAS JUNE 16, 1950, when Paul Mathis and Lily Betbeder—both riders from the Cyclo Club Béarnais in Pau—set off pedaling from the Mediterranean town of Cerbère with a plan to ride the length of the Pyrénées, their eyes set on Hendaye on the Atlantic Coast. Between them and their goal 720 kilometers (447 miles) away was the small matter of riding 11,000 meters (36,000 feet) of cols, including Col d'Aubisque, Col du Tourmalet, Col d'Aspin, and Col de Peyresourde—names that will be familiar to even a passing follower of the Tour de France.

Hidden away on the Cyclo Club Béarnais website is a description of the ride by Mathis. There he recounts the searing heat of the daytime, brutal afternoon storms, and the bitter cold across the high Pyrénéan passes; utter exhaustion and the restorative powers of salty soup and lemonade; near failure and ultimate success.

It was on the mighty Tourmalet that Mathis's attempt almost came to an

THE RAID LINKS TOGETHER 28 FAMOUS PUNCHY PYRENEAN PASSES—IT'S A CHALLENGING BUT REWARDING ROUTE.

end. Vomiting at the side of the road, and no longer able to turn his legs, he made the decision to turn around and rest, while Betbeder continued onwards. After resting for a few hours, Mathis attempted the climb again, before riding through the night—descending the Col d'Aubisque in the pitch dark—to reunite with Betbeder for their last leg. They completed what Mathis described as a "Raid Pyrénéan" on June 19.

It is a feat that is now repeated by hundreds of riders each year, either as a formal randonnée or audax. They seek to complete the route—now usually ridden in the opposite direction—within 100 hours, or as a more relaxed tour. →

CLASSIC PYRENEAN VILLAGES, STEEPED IN CYCLING CULTURE, DOT THE MOUNTAINOUS BORDERLANDS BETWEEN THE ATLANTIC AND MEDITERRANEAN.

For those completing the randonnée, it is a throwback to an era before GPS computers and trackers—they record their route via a brevet card (or "carnet" in Raid parlance), getting proofs of presence from participating establishments (contrôles) along the route. In fact, regardless of how you choose to ride the Raid, it is impossible to escape the feeling of immersion in cycling history.

On arrival in Sainte-Marie-de-Campan—at the bottom of the long, long descent from the top of the Tourmalet—you will hopefully be in slightly better shape than Eugène Christophe was during the 1913 Tour de France. Christophe was leading the race when the fork of his Peugeot bike snapped on the perilous plummet. Desperate to continue, he found a blacksmith and—in accordance with the then rules of self-sufficiency—welded a repair in order to continue. It took three hours, by which point the race was lost, and to add insult to injury, Christophe was fined even more time after officials decreed that he had received assistance from a young boy who operated the bellows while Christophe worked.

For those of us who aren't under the same time pressures as the pro-peloton, it's hard not to be lured into long lunches and café breaks along the route and the inevitable "café legs" up the next climb. The Pyrénées are famed for steeper climbs than their alpine counterparts, and gradients frequently tip into double-figure percentages. As a trade-off, the route is almost entirely on quiet roads; you are often more likely to encounter a fellow cyclist than you are a vehicle. Each climb has its own distinct feel: there's the steady but unrelenting Aubisque with long sweeping views in good weather, but little in the way of shelter should an afternoon storm roll through. Then there's the punchy Col de Portet d'Aspet whose summit barely breaks free of the shady forests that cool its lower slopes.

Despite their majesty, there are few riders who will be disappointed to be leaving the sawtooth profile of the mountains as the route mellows toward its eastern end, eyes set on the coast and the finish in Cerbère. Those who reach it do so safe in the knowledge that they've added their own name to a very tiny piece of cycling history. ○

ROUTE NOTES

Start: Hendaye, France / **Finish:** Cerbère, France / **Distance:** 720 km (447 mi) / **Duration:** 3–10 days / **Category:** Historic randonnée / **Terrain:** Tarmac / **Level:** Moderate

HIGHLIGHTS:

Before you even reach the mountains, the Corniche coastal road is a stunning farewell to the Atlantic. The summit of each and every col will be welcomed and mentally ticked off along the journey east. And any ride that finishes with a dip in the sea is a good one.

LOCAL SPECIALTIES:

Gâteau Basque may as well have been designed for hungry cyclists looking for a sugar hit. Rarely will a chilled Orangina taste as good as halfway through a hot day in the saddle. The Pyrénées region has excellent wines. How much you enjoy drinking during the ride is up to you …

WILDLIFE AND LANDSCAPE:

In good weather, expect epic views of the snowcapped peaks of the Hautes-Pyrénées.

RESUPPLY NOTES:

The route passes through towns frequently and regularly, with options ranging from restaurants to grocery stores.

ACCOMMODATIONS:

It is probably more normal for riders completing the route to do it in credit card-style, staying in hotels along the route. There are plenty of options and most are used to catering to cyclists. If you want to travel even lighter, there are lots of tour providers who will shuttle bags between accommodations and arrange bookings.

GETTING THERE (AND BACK):

Biarritz is the closest airport to the starting point, while Perpignan is easily reachable from Cerbère.

RIDE SEASON:

June to September. In general, expect high temperatures in the valleys during the day, but with potential afternoon storms and significantly colder temperatures on cols.

EQUIPMENT:

As much or as little as you like, but you are likely to be thankful for a minimalist approach on the climbs. Bring enough clothing layers to deal with the extremes of weather.

WHAT TO RIDE:

A road bike. You may want to add some easier gearing to make the steep climbs a little less painful.

OTHER IMPORTANT INFORMATION:

A number of subtle variations on the route exist. Cyclo Club Béarnais themselves publicize two options: the 720 km (447 mi) randonneur with 18 cols or the 800 km (500 mi) touriste which takes in a further 10 cols along the route.

ROUTEMAKER:

Maurice Bugard, then president of Cyclo Club Béarnais, was the first to plot a cycling route across the Pyrénées in 1912. The outbreak of war meant that he was never able to ride his vision.

CONTRIBUTOR INFO:

Tom Hardie is a cyclist and bikepacker based in London, U.K.

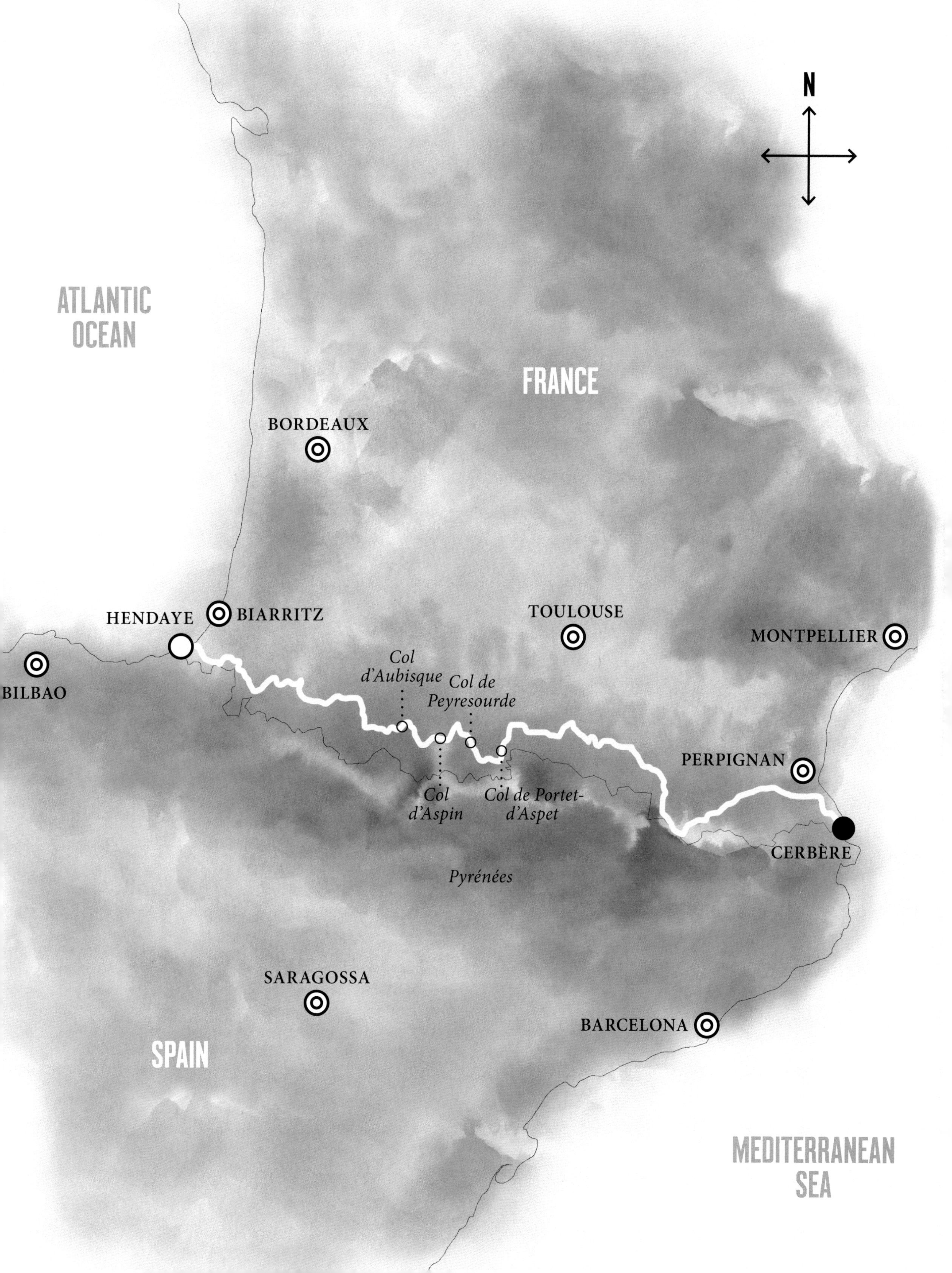
N
ATLANTIC
OCEAN
FRANCE
BORDEAUX
HENDAYE
BIARRITZ
TOULOUSE
MONTPELLIER
BILBAO
Col
d'Aubisque
Col de
Peyresourde
Col
d'Aspin
Col de Portet-
d'Aspet
PERPIGNAN
CERBÈRE
Pyrénées
SARAGOSSA
BARCELONA
SPAIN
MEDITERRANEAN
SEA

BIG MOUNTAIN ADVENTURE AROUND THE ROOF OF EUROPE

ROUTE:
TOUR DU MONT BLANC

LOCATION:
FRANCE, ITALY, AND SWITZERLAND

↑ THE TMB IS MARKED, BUT TAKE MAPS OR A NAVIGATION DEVICE FOR THE BIKEPACKING ROUTE.
→ THE ALPINE TERRAIN DEFINITELY CALLS FOR A MOUNTAIN BIKE AND PACKING LIGHT.

"JUST KEEP MONT BLANC TO YOUR RIGHT," are the most basic of route directions to give someone starting out in Chamonix, Les Houches, or Courmayeur on this challenging classic. Looping the vast, inaccessible, granite and snow-covered spine of the Mont Blanc massif, the Tour du Mont Blanc (TMB) really does pack a rewarding punch—everything from lush alpine-meadow singletrack, to harsh granite col-crushing hike-a-bike through France, Italy, and Switzerland.

As bikepacking playgrounds go, it doesn't get much better: the experience of alpinism and high-mountain culture without the need for ropes, harnesses, and crampons. Trevor Worsey, who rode the route with his partner a couple of years ago on loaded full-suspension mountain bikes, describes the TMB and its massif surrounds as "the church of open sky"—a church whose sea of contours, traversing tracks and trails, and picture-perfect postcard vistas define epic bikepacking. Riding on the shoulders of giants, however, should not be underestimated—the route is testing and challenging (more than 8,000 meters/26,000 feet of ascent over 175 kilometers/109 miles), so be prepared and modest with daily distances and expectations. Days in the mountains are as much about just being among this peak theater as it is out-and-out bikepacking; a showcase for bikes as tools for adventure. A popular hiking route too (the biking one deviates slightly), walkers opt to complete the TMB counterclockwise, but the general consensus for bikes is clockwise—not just to prevent clogging the trails but because, on a bike, the climbs/descents that way round are a little more rideable.

Despite the popularity of the route, you can still escape the crowds. In 1939, prescient mountain author R.L.G. Irving wrote, "the more that social life develops, the greater will become the need for occasional times of solitude"—and the Alps deliver in abundance. "How much more Mont Blanc means to this generation than when Horace Bénédict de Saussure visited and hiked around Mont Blanc in 1767..." he goes on, "... it had hardly ceased to be known as Mount Maudit—the Accursed Mountain—and yet Mont Blanc is now a personality →

A NETWORK OF MOUNTAIN HUTS (REFUGES/RIFUGIOS) THAT DOT THE TMB PROVIDE BASIC ACCOMMODATION AND FOOD, BUT CAMPING IS STILL AN OPTION.

"IT WAS A THRILL RIDE OF EMOTIONS, SOME ELATING, SOME EXHILARATING, AND SOME JUST BRUTALLY EXHAUSTING."

with a long history." Incentivized by geology, science, and botany, Saussure and his large team, including Michel-Gabriel Paccard and Jacques Balmat, are credited as the first to climb the 4,809-meter (15,778-foot) mountain—the highest in Europe—in 1786. Their climb is widely regarded as the birth of alpinism and the concept of the TMB was established in 1758. It became an official Grande Randonnée (GR) route in the 1950s. As a result, black-and-yellow painted signs will largely guide you now. As you spot them out of the corner of your eye, as your pedal sails past the rock one is etched on, you get some reassurance that you are on the right track. Even when you can't quite see the peak, Mont Blanc is always there; a magnet that draws you to Savoie and the TMB in the first place, then pulls you around the loop. That said, the other peaks on the ridgeline are equally spectacular with as much history to delve into—the view over to Grandes Jorasses (4,208 meters/13,806 feet) from Val Ferret and the traversing singletrack around the Bonatti Hut is sublime. Look hard enough at night, and you'll see the twinkling lights of *bivacchi* huts and climbers' headlamps.

Much like a roller coaster, there were highs and lows for Trevor: "It was a thrill ride of emotions, some elating, some exhilarating, and some just brutally exhausting," he says. "We saw Mont Blanc and its beauty, we traveled under hanging glaciers, and our bags bounced wildly as we careened down the exposed mountain track of the 2,490-meter (8,169-foot) Col Ferret. Each horizon offers new hope." ○

THE VAST, SNOW-COVERED SPINE OF THE MONT BLANC MASSIF IS NEVER OUT MIND OR OUT OF SIGHT—JUST KEEP IT ON YOUR RIGHT.

ROUTE NOTES

Start and Finish: The official start is Les Houches, but Chamonix is the most connected. Courmayeur works too. / **Distance:** 175 km (108 mi) / **Duration:** 3–6 days / **Category:** Classic mountain-biking and hiking route / **Terrain:** 50 % roads/gravel tracks, 50 % singletrack / **Level:** Difficult

LOCAL SPECIALTIES:

Hearty mountain food at the huts: polenta, fondue, and tartiflette, washed down with a local Génépi liquor. In the towns/villages you'll find pizza, espresso, pastries, and maybe even a big bikepacker bag of *chouquettes*.

WILDLIFE AND LANDSCAPE:

Much of the TMB lies above the treeline, so expect big granite peaks filling the horizon. Ride among chamois, ibex, hares, and cowbell-clanging alpine herds. You might spot marmots playing hide-and-seek amid the rocky terrain—although you're more likely to hear their loud shrills. There are too many beautiful flowers to name, but look out for edelweiss and wild thyme.

RESUPPLY NOTES:

Small villages, towns, and rifugios (mountain huts) along the route will have you covered for basic supplies, food, and drink. But it is well worth roughly planning out your daily stages and resupplies in the mountains. There is plenty of water around—take a water filter and you can enjoy the massif's meltwaters.

ACCOMMODATIONS:

This route is made for hut-to-hut bikepacking. Travel light between the great established network of mountain huts. If you want the freedom (and burden) of camping, be aware that wild camping isn't technically legal in the mountains, but it is possible providing you stick to the "leave no trace" rules and pitch somewhere safe and away from tracks and trails, between dusk and dawn. Alternative accommodation can be found in the bigger centers along the route. In high season (the only time the route is passable), it is best to book in advance.

GETTING THERE (AND BACK):

Geneva is the closest main city transport hub. Chamonix and Les Houches have train stations, but the nearest to Courmayeur is Aosta. As usual, buses will connect you if needed.

RIDE SEASON AND CLIMATE:

Snow makes the majority of the Tour du Mont Blanc impassable most of the year. The TMB window is from late June to September only, or October if the snow hasn't arrived by then. Watch out for cooler temperatures at higher altitudes, and afternoon/evening storms—especially if it's been hot and humid during the day. Before planning, check the dates of mass-participation events (like the Ultra-Trail du Mont Blanc) as it is worth avoiding those for trail and hut freedom.

EQUIPMENT:

A challenging route and plenty of rifugios lends itself to bikepacking light in true alpinist style, but ride it with full camping and cooking kit if you dare. Even if staying in huts, make sure to take a sleeping liner in case. Leave space in your bags for snacks and high-mountain layers, and don't forget riding shoes you can walk in.

WHAT TO RIDE:

The TMB is a balancing act between riding and hike-a-biking. A hardtail or full-suspension mountain bike is the best machine for the route. You can do it on a gravel bike, but be prepared to walk more, for longer sections. Easy gearing is essential if you want to ride the majority of the route, especially with a loaded bike.

CONTRIBUTOR INFO:

Having raced bikes downhill in the early days of the Enduro World Series (EWS), Trevor Worsey is a specialist when it comes to steep and demanding trails. He now spends his days running the Kids Ride Shotgun brand, bikepacking, riding trails and gravel loops, surfing, skiing, or canoeing with his young family and two dogs.

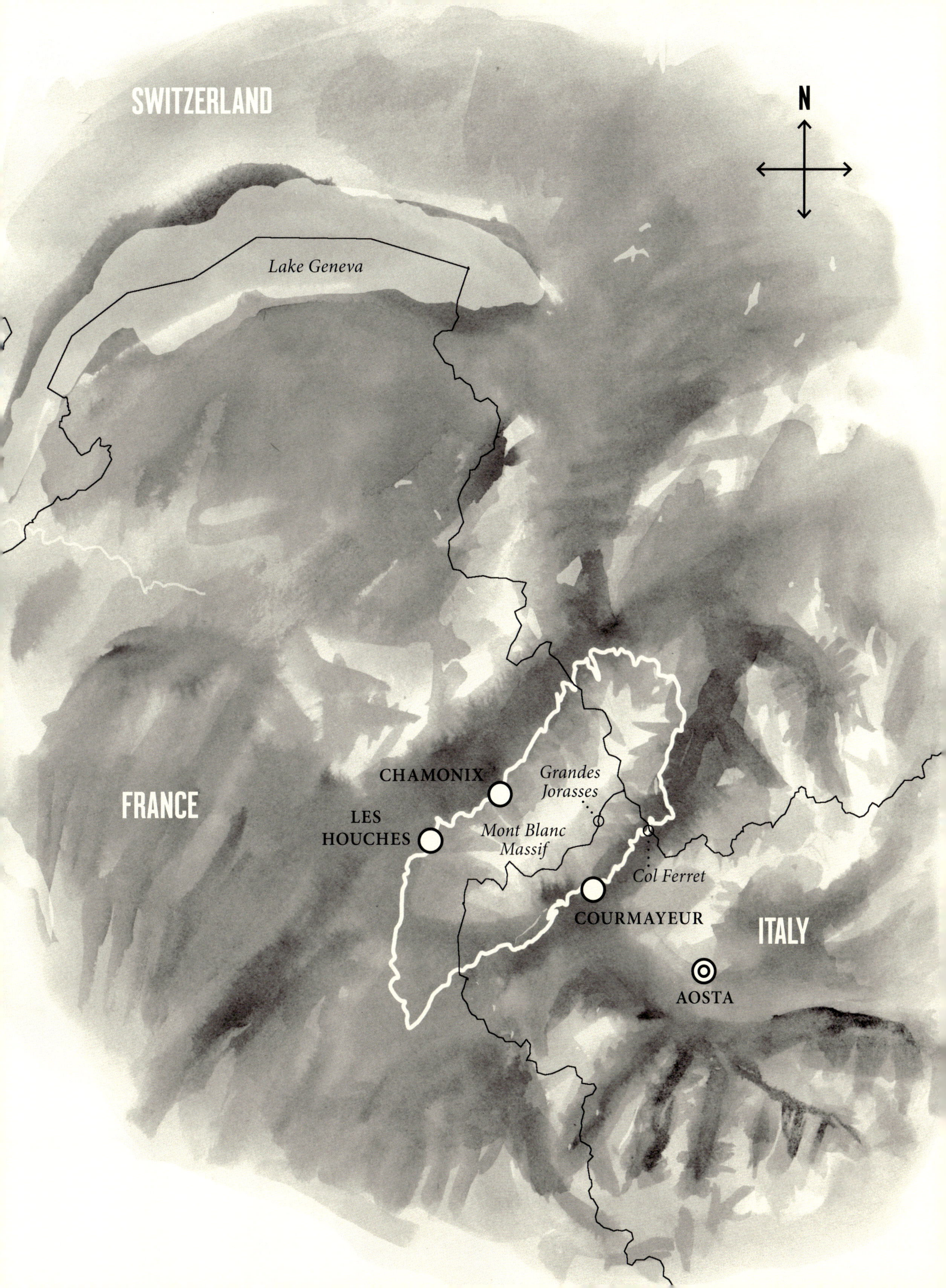
SWITZERLAND
N
Lake Geneva
CHAMONIX
Grandes Jorasses
FRANCE
LES HOUCHES
Mont Blanc Massif
Col Ferret
COURMAYEUR
ITALY
AOSTA

MOONSCAPES AND HUTS IN A LAND TIME FORGOT

ROUTE:
GR247

LOCATION:
SPAIN

"THE GR247 COMPLETELY STOLE MY HEART." It's fair to say British adventurer Katie-Jane L'Herpiniere has a pretty high bar when it comes to gnarly trips, having become the first person to walk the 4,500-kilometer (2,796-mile) Great Wall of China unsupported and ride the original 1911 Tour de France (5,439-kilometer/3,380-mile) route, again unsupported. She was also one of just 29 riders to finish the inaugural, and notoriously difficult, 1,800-kilometer (1,119-mile) Silk Road Mountain Race in Kyrgyzstan.

However, it was a little (by comparison) 330-kilometer (205-mile) loop in Andalusia that began her love affair with Southern Spain—mainly because it was unlike anything she had ridden before. That's hardly surprising given the GR247's incredible variation in landscape and terrain. In the Sierra de Cazorla and the Sierra de Segura, the days are filled with limestone gorges, while the lunar landscapes of Los Campos de Hernán Perea feel a little like riding on the moon. This is a land that time forgot: breathtaking, rugged, and, most of the time, all yours.

It was created for hikers and cyclists—and often a bit of both—and is a designated GR (Gran Recorrido) footpath. Craggy, remote, and super-demanding, there is nearly 10,000 meters (32,808 feet) of climbing across the route. In one breath, you need to be fit and fearsome to take it on, especially in summer when water resupply can be a real issue. But at the same time, the regular refugios/mountain huts (11 in total) dotted along the route mean that shelter is rarely something you need to worry about, or crucially, carry any of the heavy stuff for.

With the huts containing sleeping platforms, foldable tables, and sometimes even well water pumps, your sleeping setup could be as simple as a sleeping bag and a mat. The fueling strategy is similarly modest: carbohydrates—plenty and often. Ride to the nearest town—there aren't many, but nearly all are historic, beautiful, and memorable, especially 2,000-years-old Cazorla with its narrow streets and the ruined cathedral—head straight into the nearest *panadería* (bakery) to stock up on trail snacks, then hit the nearest restaurant/bar for carbohydrate round two. Katie-Jane picks up the story: "In addition to eating my body weight in *patatas bravas* at any given opportunity, I also couldn't get enough of the simple yet delicious *tostada con tomate* (tomatoes on bread)."

Pan-fueled perhaps but certainly not pan flat. The GR247 usually takes around a week to ride and is split into 21 stages, each between 10–20 kilometers (6–12 miles) in length. Almost all of the route is rideable, but there are some long steep hike-a-bike sections that push even the hardiest bikepacker like Katie-Jane. It's a measure of their difficulty that Tom Farrell and Laura →

"IT'S A TRIP WE WILL REMEMBER FOR THE REST OF OUR LIVES. THE MAP WE BOUGHT IS FRAMED ABOVE OUR BED."

← THE SIERRA DE CAZORLA AND SIERRA DE SEGURA OFFER BIKEPACKERS A REAL SENSE OF ESCAPE.
→ DESIGNED FOR HIKERS AND BIKERS ALIKE, EXPECT SOME CHALLENGING TERRAIN.
↓ KNOWN TO SOME AS THE "BOSQUES DEL SUR" TRAIL, THE STUNNING FORESTS OFFER GREAT CONTRAST (AND SHADE IN THE HEAT OF THE DAY).

Spinney, from the Woods Cyclery in England's New Forest, warn that it's hard to predict 100 percent which refugio you'll make it to each day, even with the relatively modest distances between them on paper.

Tom and Laura navigated on paper, but there are GPX files available for the route, which is a mix of remote gravel and technical singletrack (10 percent). It is generally ridden counterclockwise, starting and finishing in Siles, 300 kilometers (186 miles) southeast of Madrid. However, there's nothing to stop you from riding clockwise—or indeed adding on some additional miles, whether they be small local loops or linking up with another huge challenge such as Transnevada (an iconic off-road route also in Andalusia).

Historic small towns such as Cazorla, Hornos, and Pontón Bajo are a must-see and shouldn't be missed. In general though, the towns are not the reason you ride the GR247. It's the wilderness. The Sierra de Cazorla has some of the best views in Southern Spain—and, according to Katie-Jane, some of the best gravel riding in the world. On Los Campos de Hernán Perea plateau, it is easy to forget you are riding at 1,600 meters (5,249 feet) given the huge mountains on your right and left, including Calar de las Palomas and Pinar del Risco. In winter, there's every chance this part of the route will be snow covered.

However and whenever the GR247 is covered, it will leave a permanent mark. For Katie-Jane, it occupies a special place in her heart. For Tom and Laura? A place on their bedroom wall. "It's a trip we will remember for the rest of our lives," they say. "The map we bought off Spanish eBay is framed above our bed." ○

GRAVEL RIDING PARADISE, THROUGH THE GR247'S LUNAR LANDSCAPES.

ANDALUSIAN TOWNS AND VILLAGES ARE FEW AND FAR BETWEEN, BUT OFFER A CHANCE TO EAT GOOD FOOD, RESUPPLY, AND SPEND THE NIGHT.

ROUTE NOTES

Start and Finish: Siles, Spain / **Distance:** 330 km (205 mi) / **Duration:** 5–7 days / **Category:** Multiday circuit / **Terrain:** 95 % off-road / **Level:** Moderate-Difficult

LOCAL SPECIALTIES:

Panaderías (aka bakeries) are plentiful and offer perfect ride fuel: cheap and carbohydrate-heavy—what's not to like? It's worth noting that there are only a handful of towns with big-shop supermarket options. Skipping one of those is not really an option. Neither is it wise not to fill up your bidons at every single village.

WILDLIFE AND LANDSCAPE:

The landscape is as remote as it is varied. One minute it feels like you are in the desert, the next you're riding through a valley that could be in the Scottish Highlands. In the Sierra de Cazorla, don't get too caught up in some of the best gravel riding around—be sure to also watch out for griffon vultures. They were the only company L'Herpiniere had when she rode through.

RESUPPLY NOTES:

Water is not plentiful, especially in summer. If there is a water pump, and it's working, it's a bonus rather than something to rely on. Each town usually has a market, but be aware that out of season, for example in winter, a lot of the resupply options are closed.

ACCOMMODATIONS:

The GR247 is nirvana for bikepackers who like to sleep out, but don't want to be put out by carrying a tent. The 11 *refugios* (mountain huts) on the route have sleeping platforms, meaning all you need is a sleeping bag, and a mat if you like a bit of comfort. The huts are not the only option. Most of the smaller towns have basic hostel-style accommodations.

GETTING THERE (AND BACK):

Madrid airport is 300 km (186 mi) and a three-hour drive away. You can get a train from Madrid to Jodar-Ubeda, but that is still 50 km (31 mi) from Cazorla, although you can ride some excellent gravel roads to get there as a warm-up if your legs are feeling good.

RIDE SEASON:

Summer is hot, dry, and probably best avoided, not least because of the lack of water. Even in early September, a lot of the springs are likely to be dry. Spring and fall are ideal. The Sierra de Cazorla is one of the rainiest places in Southern Spain. Peak rainfall? Late November to early February. And when it rains, it really comes down. The mud will stick to your bike "like concrete," according to L'Herpiniere.

EQUIPMENT:

Outside of summer, the nights will be chilly so you'll need a down jacket and a warm sleeping bag. In general, the proliferation of mountain huts means you just need a sleeping bag and a mat. Going light on the sleeping setup means you'll have plenty of room for water—make use of it.

WHAT TO RIDE:

A mountain-bike with suspension, ideally. It could also be ridden on a gravel bike. Whatever you choose, be prepared to walk—and carry—your steed. Some sections are so steep that it's almost impossible to ride.

CONTRIBUTOR INFO:

Tom Farrell and Laura Spinney from the Woods Cyclery and British adventurer Katie-Jane L'Herpiniere.

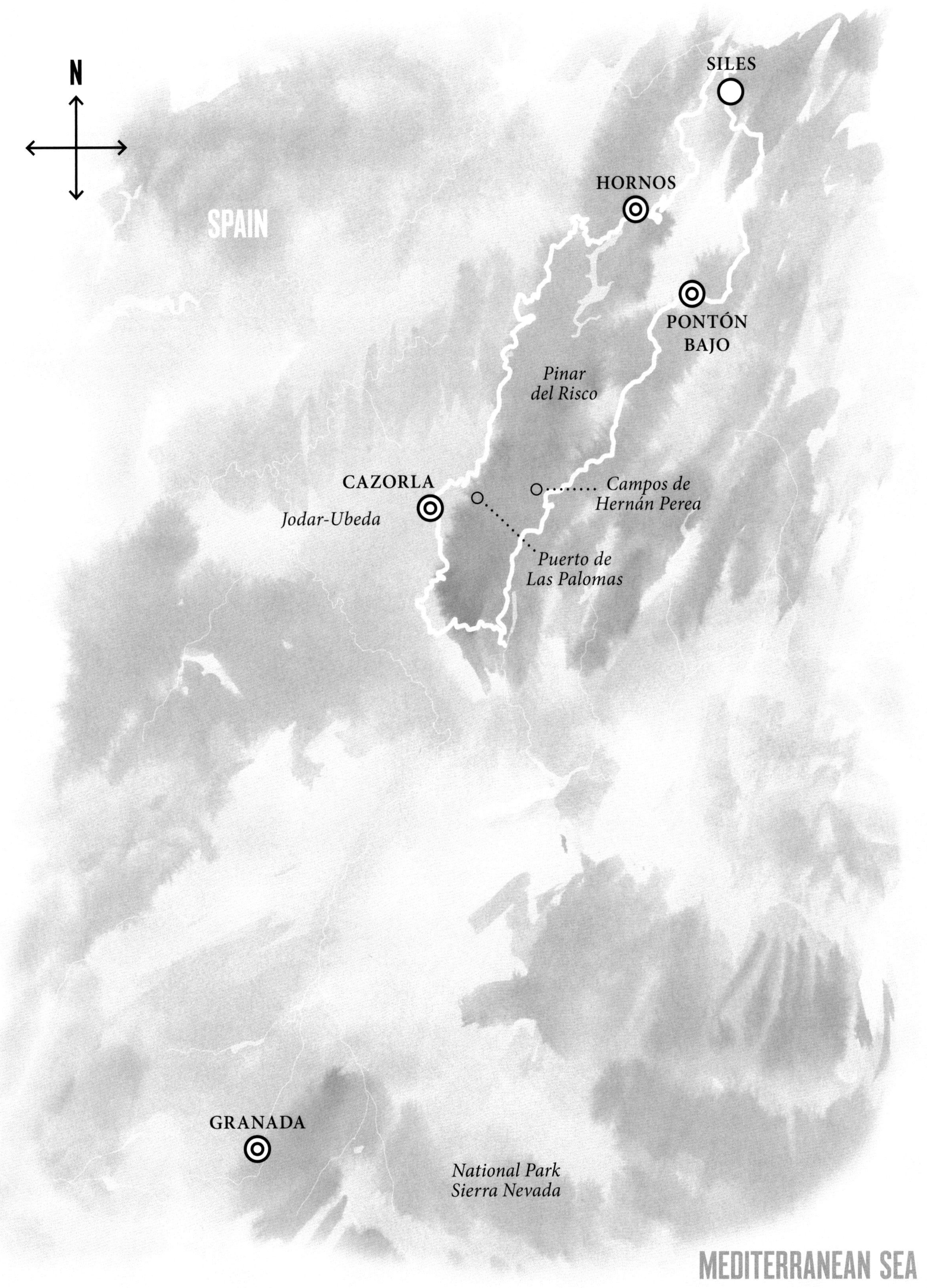
N
SILES
HORNOS
SPAIN
PONTÓN
BAJO
Pinar
del Risco
CAZORLA
Campos de
Hernán Perea
Jodar-Ubeda
Puerto de
Las Palomas
GRANADA
National Park
Sierra Nevada
MEDITERRANEAN SEA

CONNECTING THE CANARY ISLANDS

ROUTE:
GRANGUANCHE

LOCATION:
CANARY ISLANDS, SPAIN

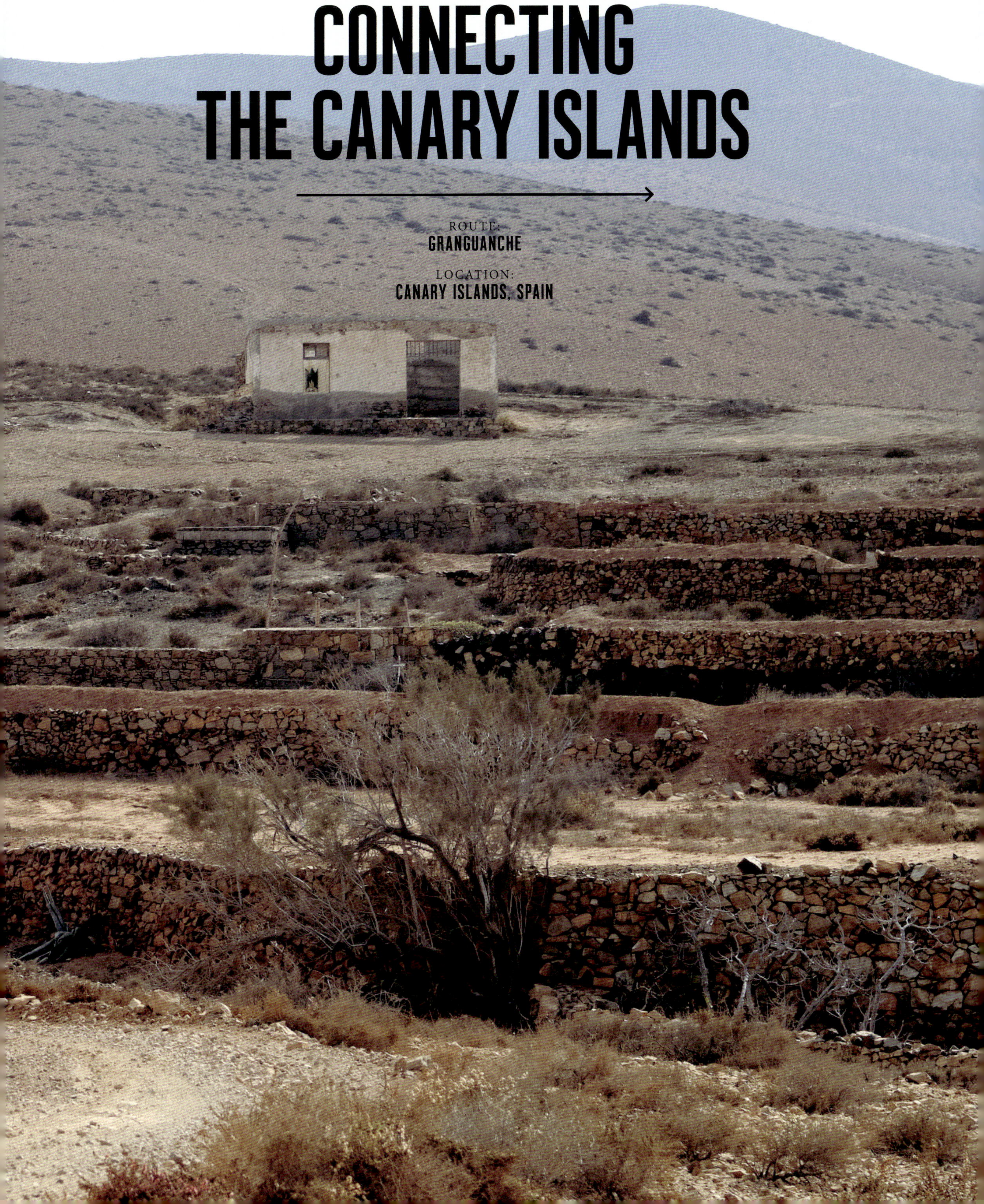

THE CANARY ISLANDS are so much more than sun and sea and beach holidays. The GranGuanche route is designed to showcase everything else the Atlantic archipelago has to offer. The route is relatively new, and was designed by Matteo Minelli, using his local knowledge to combine sections of the GR131 walking path with logical linking sections to create an island traverse from the northeastern tip of Lanzarote to the western tip of Tenerife.

Taking inspiration from routes like the Torino-Nice Rally, the GranGuanche blends adventure and magnificent landscapes with regular sorties into local towns and villages. But what maybe sets GranGuanche apart from its inspiration is the rich variety of terrain, views, and subtle changes of culture that each island brings. Lanzarote, Fuerteventura, Gran Canaria, Tenerife, and El Hierro each has its defining features and unique ambiance.

Ask most who complete the annual organized Audax ride of the route and they will have little to tell you about Lanzarote, as the event sets off at 10:00 p.m. They miss out on lava fields and moon-like terrain, vineyards and black sandy beaches as they blast along the 110 kilometers (68 miles) to Playa Blanca. Fuerteventura brings with it precipitous coastal cliffs, rich orange-tinged desert-like ridgelines, and the historic town of Betancuria—the oldest Spanish town on the archipelago.

The mountainous north of Gran Canaria possesses its own microclimate. More humid and prone to rain, the route passes through Jurassic Park-style foliage and high pine forests—a stark contrast to the arid plains →

HOPPING BETWEEN THE CANARY ISLANDS, THIS ROUTE IS NAMED AFTER THE GUANCHES, THE FIRST INDIGENOUS GROUP TO SETTLE HERE FROM THE AFRICAN MAINLAND.

that have gone before. The spherical military radar station at Pico de las Nieves marks the high point of the island and the start of a long descent through bizarre rock formations.

It would be unfair to reduce Tenerife to the volcano of Mount Teide, but it looms in waiting for riders as they climb through rock-strewn flanks interspersed with scrubby brush and cacti on its lower slopes.

Finally, El Hierro—a bonus loop, but with a sting in the tail: 4,000 meters (13,000 feet) of climbing on a 120-kilometer (71-mile) lap of the island. The climbs are steeper, descents rougher, and gravel looser. In fact, the whole island feels a little wilder, as though it is set on the edge of the world. It would be easy to imagine "here be monsters" scrawled on old maps and if you squint, the wind-shaped juniper trees look like strange beasts grasping at some invisible quarry.

Riding GranGuanche is like reading a book or possibly even an entire library of books. If each island represents a chapter or volume contributing to a longer tale, the ferry journeys act as a convenient bookmark. They are an enforced break—time to refuel and rest, but also time to reflect and digest what has gone before and what is to come. They also bring with them their own challenges. Do you race through the final pages of each route, in the hope of leaping straight onto the ferry and continuing apace? Maybe there is more to be gained by embracing the rigidities of the timetable and luxuriating in a more gentle pace, paying a little more attention to the world through which you are passing.

No matter how quickly you choose to travel, you will experience the sea crossings at the same speed, the open North Atlantic Ocean rocking and rolling—the means by which Spanish explorers first "discovered" the Canaries. Except, of course, they had been inhabited for at least a thousand years before that date. The GranGuanche pays tribute to the original aboriginal settlers of the islands, the Guanches. And that feels apt, because at its soul, the ride is not about conquering a route, it is about immersing yourself in the landscape and heritage of each distinct place—a true journey of discovery. ○

"THE RIDE IS NOT ABOUT CONQUERING A ROUTE, IT IS ABOUT IMMERSING YOURSELF IN THE LANDSCAPE AND HERITAGE OF EACH DISTINCT PLACE."

← THERE ARE THREE ROUTE OPTIONS FOR ROAD, GRAVEL, AND MOUNTAIN (TRAIL) BIKES.
→ LUSH GREEN FOREST BLANKETS THE ARCHIPELAGO, USUALLY SHROUDED IN ENCHANTING MIST.
↓ CAMPING ISN'T WIDELY ACCESSIBLE IN THE CANARY ISLANDS, SO RIDE LIGHT AND SEEK ACCOMMODATION.

EACH ISLAND HAS ITS OWN CHARACTER—FROM THE BLACK LAVA FIELDS OF LANZAROTE, TO THE MT. TEIDE (3,715 M/12,188 FT) HIGH POINT ON TENERIFE, TO THE WHITE SAND BEACHES OF FUERTEVENTURA.

"THE GRANGUANCHE BLENDS ADVENTURE AND MAGNIFICENT LANDSCAPES WITH REGULAR SORTIES INTO LOCAL TOWNS AND VILLAGES."

ROUTE NOTES

Start: Órzola, Lanzarote / **Finish:** Los Cristianos, Tenerife / **Distance:** 700 km (435 mi) / **Duration:** 4–10 days / **Category:** Multiday, point-to-point / **Terrain:** Gravel – 70 % unpaved / **Level:** Intermediate

HIGHLIGHTS:

Escaping the tourist hotspots for a true insight into the beauty of the Canary Islands. Each rider will have their own personal favorite island and linking the route by ferry creates a unique journey.

LOCAL SPECIALTIES:

Bocadillos stuffed with local seafood and the Canary Island delicacy of papas arrugadas—new potatoes boiled in seawater—are the perfect bikepacking energy food.

WILDLIFE AND LANDSCAPE:

The route passes through wildly differing landscapes from beaches to deserts, volcanic landscapes, and jungle-like canyons.

RESUPPLY NOTES:

The route passes through many towns, including ferry ports. It is very possible to complete the route without a stove, making use of restaurants and grocery stores. As always, keep an eye on the route profile and be sure to have enough food and water for each section.

ACCOMMODATIONS:

There are limited legal camping options on the island. If you are forced to sleep in the wild, arrive late, leave early, and don't light a fire. There are plenty of hotels along the route, and it is possible to complete it without sleeping outside.

GETTING THERE (AND BACK):

Órzola is a short ride from Lanzarote Airport. At the other end, Tenerife South Airport is near the finish. It is possible to buy a cardboard bike box from Bike Point in Playa de las Américas. It is a 20-minute taxi ride from there to the airport.

RIDE SEASON AND CLIMATE:

It is possible to complete the ride at any time of year. Spring and fall offer optimal conditions, with average temperatures between 15–25 °C (59–77 °F). Expect the odd colder day in winter, and summer can be stiflingly hot away from the coast or mountain peaks. It is possible to have cold weather and even freezing conditions almost any time of year at the highest points of the ride. The prevailing winds blow from north to south. It's therefore recommended to ride the route in that direction.

EQUIPMENT:

No specific equipment is required. Ensure you have sufficient water carrying capacity for a long day. A GPS device will make navigation significantly easier. Don't forget your sunscreen!

WHAT TO RIDE:

The gravel GranGuanche route is tailor-made for gravel bikes, although could be completed on a mountain bike.

OTHER IMPORTANT INFORMATION:

It is possible to add a bonus island, La Graciosa, at the start of the route, or forgo the loop of El Hierro at the end. The route is dependent on ferry travel between islands. Ferry crossings can be rough, so bring seasick medication if you are prone to feeling queasy. Check timetables to ensure you are not left waiting too long at ports (or make the most of a wait in a local bar!). The total cost of ferry travel is around €200 ($215).

ROUTEMAKER:

GranGuanche was created by Matteo Minelli.

CONTRIBUTOR INFO:

Italian Matteo Minelli has lived in the Canary Islands since 2014 and is a passionate promoter of the gravel riding. Alice Simpkins-Woods is a gravel rider based in the U.K. The GranGuanche was her first bikepacking ride abroad.

CANARY ISLANDS
LA GRACIOSA
LANZAROTE
ÓRZOLA
LA PALMA
TENERIFE
BETANCURIA
FUERTEVENTURA
Mount Teide
LOS CRISTIANOS
LA GOMERA
EL HIERRO
Pico de las Nieves
GRAN CANARIA
ATLANTIC OCEAN
MOROCCO
N
ALGERIA

COAST AND RIDGE LANDS ALONG THE ADRIATIC

ROUTE:
ADRIATIC CREST

LOCATION:
CROATIA

A GOOD MIX OF QUIET ROADS AND GRAVEL TRACKS LEAD BIKEPACKERS INLAND AND UP INTO THE LESSER-DISCOVERED CROATIAN BACKCOUNTRY.

THE ADRIATIC CREST traces its namesake coastline, but rather than sticking to the beaches and seafront tourist hotspots, it takes to the mountains, leaving behind the well-trodden paths to discover a side of Croatia that is rarely seen by visitors. It is a land of wild contrasts, from sleepy farming communities with stacked white-stone houses, to historic towns with still-visible scars of conflict, and rocky, bruising trails.

The "official" start of the route lies just over the Slovenian border in the mountains, where it picks its way along ridges and through valleys before descending down to the first sea crossing of the journey, to the islands of Cres and Krk. The islands have been claimed by, among others, the ancient Greeks, the Romans, the Byzantine Empire, Croatian counts and kings, the Venetian Empire, the Napoleonic French Empire, and, in the 20th century, were occupied by both Italian and German forces. Without wanting to trivialize two millennia of politics and power struggles, it is not hard to see why so many powers wanted to lay claim to such beautiful islands, surrounded by the deepest azure seas imaginable.

Back on the mainland, the route enters the Northern Velebit National Park. The Velebit Mountains are not the highest range in Croatia, but they are the largest. As you leave the sea behind, the trail snakes up on soft loam through coniferous forests, accompanied by a symphonic soundtrack of birdsong. The section of trail between Kraljevica and Gospić reaches farthest into the mountains; paths are often overgrown or blocked by trees, and descents and climbs are awkward and technically hard—but the effort pays off on high ridges that offer long views across the Velebit range.

Just over halfway along the route is Gospić, the birthplace of Nikola Tesla—a statue of the inventor and early electrical pioneer stands in a square named after him. It was reinstalled in 2021 after the original was destroyed during the Croatian War of Independence (1991–1995). The town fought hard against Serbian forces and bullet-holed buildings on almost every block are a visible reminder of the conflict.

The southern stretches of the Adriatic Crest feel like a newer Croatia; one in which tourism's influence conjures plentiful gelato shops and quaint cafes. There is still an opportunity to escape the bustling crowds, however, as the trail diverts into the Krka National Park, an area with the second-highest concentration of lavender in Europe, and limestone bedrock that gives birth to deep caves and cascading waterfalls around every corner.

Gradually, lush forests give way to olive groves and vineyards. Mountain summits grant views out to scattered islands (there are over 1,000 dotted along the Adriatic coastline) and the final few miles of the route include a ferry from the island Čiovo into the center of Split. It is a perfectly apt way to complete a journey that feels defined by the sea, even on a route that deliberately deviates from the coastline. ○

THE SOUTHERN PART OF THE ROUTE OFFERS UP MUCH ROCKIER AND ARID TERRAIN THAN THE NORTH, WITH LUSH FORESTS REPLACED BY OLIVE GROVES AND VINEYARDS.

"THE EFFORT PAYS OFF ON HIGH RIDGES THAT OFFER LONG VIEWS ACROSS THE VELEBIT RANGE."

WITH A REAL MIX OF TECHNICAL OFF-ROAD RIDING AND PAVED ROADS, A MOUNTAIN BIKE IS DEFINITELY RECOMMENDED FOR THIS ROUTE.

"IT IS A PERFECTLY APT WAY
TO COMPLETE A JOURNEY
THAT FEELS DEFINED BY THE SEA."

RESUPPLY IS SPARSE; STOCK UP ON FOOD AND WATER WHEN YOU CAN. RIDE AT THE RIGHT TIME OF YEAR, AND YOU'LL HAVE THE PICKINGS OF FRESH FRUIT IN ABUNDANCE.

"IT IS A LAND OF WILD CONTRASTS, FROM SLEEPY FARMING COMMUNITIES, TO HISTORIC TOWNS, AND ROCKY, BRUISING TRAILS."

APART FROM A COUPLE OF ISLAND HOPS, THE ROUTE IS ON THE CROATIAN MAINLAND WITH THE ADRIATIC SEA AND HUNDREDS OF ISLANDS TEASING ON THE HORIZON. FINISH AT A BEACH NEAR SPLIT FOR A WELL-EARNED SWIM.

ROUTE NOTES

Start: Ilirska Bistrica, Slovenia / **Finish:** Split, Croatia / **Distance:** 612 km (380 mi) / **Duration:** 7–10 days / **Category:** Multiday point-to-point journey / **Terrain:** Rocky doubletrack and singletrack, 30 % paved / **Level:** Moderate

HIGHLIGHTS:

A museum with displays about Nikola Tesla's life—with working replicas of some of his most famous inventions—is in Smiljan (near Gospić) on the site of his childhood home. It would also be remiss not to take a dip in the Adriatic Sea or the pools formed by the waterfalls in Krka National Park.

LOCAL SPECIALTIES:

Ripe plums, apples, sweet chestnuts, and figs along the trail during summer. Big burek pasties are made of many thin layers of dough, filled with cheese or meat, and sometimes with sweet fruit fillings. It is wise to save trying *rakija* (fruit brandy) for the end of the day.

WILDLIFE AND LANDSCAPE:

See if you can spot the enormous griffon vultures swooping above Cres.

RESUPPLY NOTES:

The landscape is persistently dry and finding water can sometimes be an issue. Make sure you have the capacity to carry 4–6 liters at any one time. Use wells to keep your supply topped up. There are amazing restaurants and markets in many towns, but the middle section of the route is very sparse in terms of resources. Bring at least two days' worth of food for the 185 km (115 mi) stretch between Kraljevica and Gospić.

ACCOMMODATIONS:

The middle section of the route will require camping. Pitch up with some consideration, and you'll have no issues when wild camping.

GETTING THERE (AND BACK):

The easiest way to get to the route is to fly into Ljubljana in Slovenia. You can then catch a bike-friendly train from Ljubljana to Ilirska Bistrica.

RIDE SEASON:

May to October. Summer temperatures can be extremely hot with storms and wetter, cooler weather in the mountains.

EQUIPMENT:

Standard bikepacking and camping gear is sufficient for this route.

WHAT TO RIDE:

There isn't one perfect bike for this route. The rougher sections warrant at least a hardtail mountain bike, but there are also long sections of tarmac. While you could ride it on a gravel bike, expect it to be pretty miserable on some of the off-road segments.

OTHER IMPORTANT INFORMATION:

There are three ferry trips on the route. Sailing times can be found online.

ROUTEMAKER:

Created by cycling adventurist and bikepacker Joe Cruz.

CONTRIBUTOR INFO:

Leslie Kehmeier has been telling stories about the outdoors for over two decades.

SLOVENIA
N
LJUBLJANA
ILIRSKA BISTRICA
TRIESTE
CROATIA
ZAGREB
KRALJEVICA
KRK
CRES
Northern Velebit National Park
GOSPIĆ
BOSNIA AND HERZEGOVINA
Krka National Park
ADRIATIC SEA
SPLIT
ČIOVO

THE GIANT CHALLENGE OF ARMENIA'S LESSER CAUCASUS

ROUTE:
TRANSCAUCASIAN TRAIL (ARMENIA STAGE)

LOCATION:
ARMENIA

JAPAN: "LAND OF THE RISING SUN." USA: "Land of the free." Korea: "Land of the morning calm." These unofficial nicknames give the countries in question a big sell. They scream, more than anything else, hope. Armenia's unofficial moniker? The "country of stones." It has to be one of the most uninspiring and unfair nicknames for a country in the world. But, as we will find out, names can often be deceiving.

The Armenian leg of the Transcaucasian Trail (TCT)—a 3,000-kilometer (1,864-mile) planned route in its entirety—is a huge challenge: nearly 700 kilometers (435 miles) of often rough-and-ready terrain in unpredictable weather. But the rewards are sensational. Ancient monasteries, petroglyphs thousands of years old, nomadic shepherds, and the stunning Gegham Mountains combine to create an unforgettable few weeks in the saddle. Well, mostly in the saddle. You'll also spend a good deal of time either carrying your bike or out of the saddle given that the route has 17,975 meters (58,973 feet) of climbing.

One trip was enough to capture Chris Goodman's heart. Chris spent nearly 20 years as an environmental consultant but now spends his time riding and documenting (in words, photographs, and drone footage) his adventures around the globe. His time in Armenia was spent as part of a roughshod peloton led by Tom Allen. Allen is the founder of the TCT, a project to build a world-class trail network stretching 3,000 kilometers (1,864 miles) along the Greater and Lesser Caucasus mountains through Georgia, Armenia, and Azerbaijan.

The initiative is ongoing, but the Armenia leg is ready to be ridden. To do so, the first job is to get to Gogavan on the Georgian-Armenian border. If you have ridden through Georgia you'll have already tackled the Greater Caucasus. Next up is Armenia's Lesser Caucasus, which does not live up to its more diminutive name. Not at all. Riders will need to climb the equivalent of two full trips from sea level to the top of Mount Everest across the 698-kilometer (434-mile) route.

Mountain bikes are a must, given that the only soft part of the experience is the ubiquitous soft, thin, unleavened flatbreads (lavash) served across the country. The warmth of Armenian hospitality can be relied upon throughout. "It's common to be invited into people's homes for bread, cheeses, fresh honey, tomato and cucumber salads, walnuts, and local spirits—we had quince and pear vodka," Chris says. "At least three shots seem compulsory."

The weather though? Less welcoming. Mid-June to mid-October is best to give yourself a chance of warm weather. Goodman rode with a group of friends in September and was expecting a dry, sunny, temperate time on two wheels. "Instead we got hit by a week of freak weather with black skies and cold →

ARMENIA'S GEGHAM MOUNTAINS ARE A REMOTE CHAIN OF VOLCANIC MOUNTAINS, SURROUNDED BY HIGH-ALTITUDE GOLDEN PLATEAUS AT AN AVERAGE HEIGHT OF 2,500 M (8,200 FT) ABOVE SEA LEVEL.

rain for five days solid," he says. "This led to freezing extremities, more mud than any of us had ever seen and that at times stopped us riding or pushing, and early-stage hypothermia in one case." Later in Chris' trip, the extreme heat caused its own share of problems, speaking to the unpredictability of the former Soviet republic's weather system.

One guarantee for any rider taking on the challenge is to expect to be captivated by the Gegham Mountains. When riding through Armenia's towns and cities, accommodations are plentiful, predictable, and secured at the touch of an online booking button. In the volcanic domes of the Gegham—often more than 3,000 meters (10,000 feet) in altitude—the only company you'll have are the nomadic shepherds, drawn to the expansive grasslands. Given that they probably invented wild camping, they won't bat an eyelid if you pitch up wherever you feel. These moments, and this landscape, were the standout

few days of Chris' trip: and if the mountains feel remote, even in the busier areas, tourism is not common. English is not widely spoken outside of towns and given that Armenia has its own language and alphabet, making yourself understood can sometimes be a little bit like the path under your wheels—rocky.

Which brings us back to where we started: Armenia's nickname might need a little bit of work, but as a bikepacking challenge—culturally, athletically, and culinarily—the Lesser Caucasus packs a giant punch. ○

GOLDEN, GREEN, AND BROWN TINGED GRASSLANDS MAKE UP ARMENIA'S OTHER-WORLDLY LANDSCAPES, WITH THE SCALE HARD TO CAPTURE.

WHEN THE MOUNTAINS ARE NOT COVERED IN SNOW, NOMADS FROM THE LOWLANDS BRING THEIR LIVESTOCK ONTO THE PLAINS TO GRAZE DURING THE SUMMER MONTHS. THE YEZIDI ARE THE LARGEST MINORITY GROUP IN ARMENIA.

ROUTE NOTES

Start: Gogavan, Armenia, on the border with Georgia / **Finish:** Meghri, Amenia, on the border with Iran / **Distance:** 698 km (434 mi) / **Duration:** 14–21 days / **Category:** Multi-week traverse / **Terrain:** 80 % unpaved, 17,975 m (58,973 ft) of ascent / **Level:** Difficult

LOCAL SPECIALTIES:

Lavash—a soft unleavened flatbread—paired with pungent local cheeses, and Armenian coffee, aka *soorj*—small cups of thick, moreish Joe (no grande lattes here).

WILDLIFE AND LANDSCAPE:

The south of Armenia has bears so bear that in mind, although you're unlikely to spot one. You won't miss the wildflowers, especially in the province of Lori. They are stunning—and everywhere.

RESUPPLY NOTES:

You won't go hungry (see local specialties) or thirsty, but there are some remote sections in which you'll need to be self-sufficient for a few days. There are plenty of water taps in towns and villages, and there are rivers (take a filter though).

ACCOMMODATIONS:

The main cities you pass through have mainstream options—hotels, hostels, etc. In the higher, more remote ground, wild camping is certainly not frowned upon; there are nomadic shepherds in the area, after all.

GETTING THERE (AND BACK):

If you take on the route north-south then Tbilisi International Airport is a two-hour drive from the start at Gogavan. Nakhchivan International Airport is a similar drive from the finish in Meghri—if you don't want to carry on into Iran, that is.

RIDE SEASON AND CLIMATE:

Mid-June to mid-October is the best time to ride.

EQUIPMENT:

Clothing-wise, be prepared for all seasons. Even in summer, the weather is very changeable—Goodman experienced cold and wet weather early on before struggling in the heat two weeks in. In the Gegham Mountains, you will often be riding at over 3,000-m (10,000-ft) altitudes making warm clothes and sleeping bags a must.

WHAT TO RIDE:

Bigger-wheeled mountain bikes—29 in. hardtail or rigid. There are large stretches of tarmac but a lot of it is broken and there are also plenty of off-road sections and tracks, some of which is hike-a-bike.

ROUTEMAKER:

Cass Gilbert and Logan Watts, with a good deal of help on some sections provided by Tom Allen.

CONTRIBUTOR INFO:

Chris Goodman, a photographer, writer, bikepacker, mountain-bike leader, and drone pilot from the United Kingdom. He spent nearly 20 years as an environmental consultant but got fed up with being tied to a desk and is now "piecing together an alternative based on doing things that I love." Amen to that.

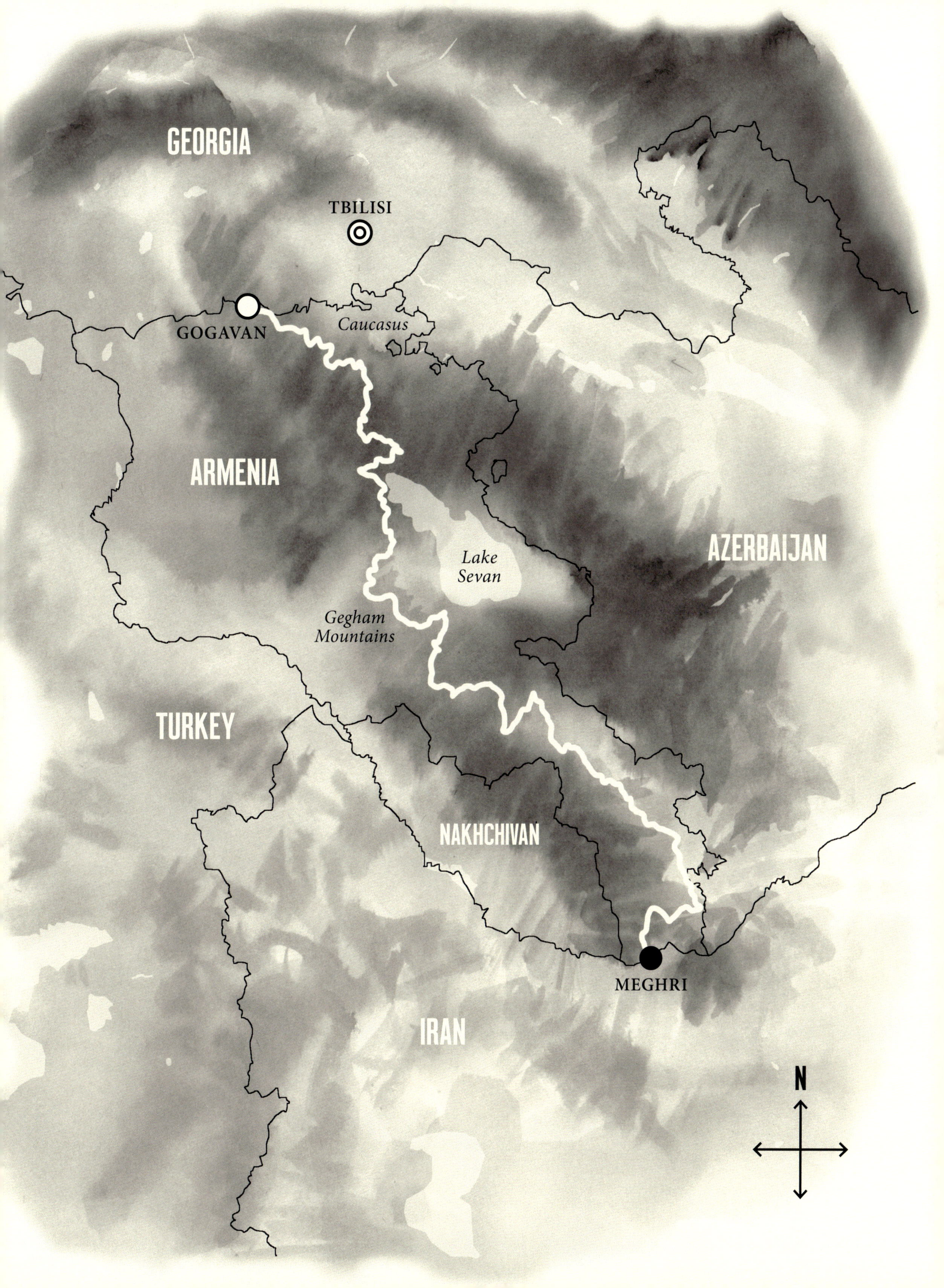
GEORGIA
TBILISI
GOGAVAN
Caucasus
ARMENIA
Lake Sevan
AZERBAIJAN
Gegham Mountains
TURKEY
NAKHCHIVAN
MEGHRI
IRAN
N

SIGNATURE BRITISH ESCAPE AMONGST SPARSE, SILENT LANDS

ROUTE:
CAIRNGORMS LOOP

LOCATION:
SCOTLAND, U.K.

THE U.K.'S HIGHEST, WILDEST, most inaccessible tract of land, boasting five of Scotland's six-highest mountains, the Cairngorms Loop of the Cairngorm Massif has become a classic bikepacking route in the Scottish Highlands, connecting glens and towns, and beautiful nothingness in between. "It's not often you can ride for a whole day without seeing a single other soul—in the U.K., anyway," says Stef Amato who traveled the route with Jordan Gibbons, and their friends Leonie and Harry, in May 2022. The main Outer Loop is a single 200-kilometer (124-mile) lap of the Cairngorms National Park. The higher, more challenging and remote Inner Loop adds a second 100-kilometer (62-mile) lap on technical mountain bike terrain.

Even at the sleepy start village of Blair Atholl, it is difficult to picture the magnitude and remoteness of the route. And yet, heading into the Cairngorms proper via the gravel doubletrack estate roads, high bogs, and loch-skirting singletrack of the Gaick Pass, you're immersed in it almost immediately. The western shore of Loch an Duin was the first obstacle on the route for Stef and his group, a couple of hours into the ride. A sea of contours around the loch—the route is a trickle of shoreline singletrack—hints at the meaning of "dùin," Scottish Gaelic for "enclosed, surrounded."

Ryvoan Bothy is a small, charming building set in a prominent position among the Abernethy Nature Reserve, in the shadows of several 800-meter (2,625-foot) peaks. Like many bothies, it was a farm building and abandoned in the late 19th century. Renovated in 1967, it is one of nearly 100 bothies that form the U.K.'s network of mountain and wilderness shelters run by an organization called the Mountain Bothies Association (MBA). Bothies aren't bookable, so knowing if you can stay in one (let alone have them to yourself) is one of life's great unknowns. But the shelter and coziness of a bothy to settle, cook, and socialize within makes a good marker in exposed lands in which, as Nan Shepherd writes of the Cairngorms, "Life has not much margin ..." Bothies are very much part of outdoor culture in the United Kingdom. These shelters, open to anyone, enable both multiday access to wild places and the most amazing locations for overnighting on bikepacking trips. "The open door of a bothy is a big hug at the end of a day's bikepacking," Stef says.

Despite being a loop, the web of interconnected glens, whose streams and rivers eventually drain into the rivers Dee and Spey, can get wonderfully disorienting, not least because you'll be regularly crossing rivers and watersheds. The mesmerizingly clear waters possess an "elemental transparency" writes Nan Shepherd in her book →

"BOTHIES ARE VERY MUCH PART OF OUTDOOR CULTURE IN THE UNITED KINGDOM. THE OPEN DOOR OF A BOTHY IS A BIG HUG AT THE END OF A DAY'S BIKEPACKING."

← A NETWORK OF GRAVEL DOUBLE-TRACK ROADS AND MOORLAND SINGLETRACK LEAD YOU ON A LAP OF THE CAIRNGORMS MASSIF.
↓ WORKING OUT OPTIONS FOR AN OVERNIGHT BOTHY STAY.

The Living Mountain, flowing from granite depths without peat to darken it. Shepherd notes, "The sound of all this moving water is as integral to the mountain as pollen to the flower. One hears it without listening as one breathes without thinking." You'll hear plenty of water on the Cairngorms Loop, whether streams rushing off the hills, or white water rushing against shins and spokes on a river crossing.

With a set of lofty, foreboding hills to your right the whole way around the loop, your eye is constantly drawn to leading lines; penetrative tracks and trails in the landscape. Heather-clad masses of granite—once higher than the →

ROUTES THROUGH THE ANCIENT CALEDONIAN PINE FORESTS OF INSHRIACH AND FESHIE MAKE FOR A SPECIAL SECTION OF THE CAIRNGORMS LOOP; PRETTY MUCH THE ONLY TREE-COVER.

"IT'S NOT OFTEN YOU CAN RIDE FOR A WHOLE DAY WITHOUT SEEING A SINGLE OTHER SOUL."

Alps—have been eroded to rounded hills, with streams and big rivers creating rifts in the plateau—rifts that happen to provide ace through routes for bikepackers. "If I had to pick a favorite section, it would be Tomintoul to Blair Atholl," Stef says. It's the perfect mix of fast-rolling road, gravel tracks, loch-skirting singletrack, climbs, descents, bothies, hike-a-bike, mild and wild, and access to the high plateau. Riding around Culardoch (900 meters/2,953 feet), you really get a sense of the Cairngorms' scale, sparsity, and silence, on top of an empty world.

Riding bikes in the Cairngorms isn't about conquering big climbs; it's about being among the mountains. The main Outer Loop is enough of a challenging bikepacking adventure, but if you want to become a true Cairngormer, take on the Inner Loop too. Either way, just go. Go to experience her tracks and trails, weathers and wildness, burns and bothies, silence and solitude. The Cairngorms Loop has everything you'd want from a bikepacking trip; it is arguably the U.K.'s finest template for an adventure by bike. And the hug of a bothy is awaiting you somewhere along the way … ○

ROUTE NOTES

Start and Finish: Blair Atholl, Scotland / **Distance:** Outer Loop (200 km/124 mi) + Inner Loop (100 km, 62 mi) / **Duration:** Outer Loop (2–4 days) + Inner Loop (3–6 days) / **Category:** Off-road bikepacking adventure / **Terrain:** 10 % asphalt, 57 % gravel/doubletrack, 33 % singletrack / **Level:** Moderate-Difficult

NOTE:

The Loop officially starts and finishes in Blair Atholl village. There are basic stores, cafes, and accommodations, and plenty more in nearby Pitlochry. Given it is a loop, you can start anywhere—Aviemore would be another good option.

LOCAL SPECIALTIES:

Venison and game. You might even spot a "deer larder" along the route. Snack-wise, macaroni pies are great, and you should dip shortbread into a camp coffee. Then there's whisky, of course. There is only one distillery along the route—Speyside distillery in Drumguish (small, private)—but fear not, there are a handful of well-known distilleries such as Glenlivet and Dalwhinnie nearby.

WILDLIFE AND LANDSCAPE:

Described as "Britain's Arctic," little other than the hardiest of low-lying plants, shrubs, and heather survives exposure on the Cairngorms high hills. On the lower slopes and wider valleys, you can find dense tree cover, some of which is ancient Caledonian Forest Scots pine. The northwestern sections of singletrack, through Inshriach and Feshie forests and around Loch an Eilein, are lovely examples. When riding, play "I-Spy" for eagles, grouse, ptarmigan, curlews, skylarks, snipes, deer, hares, and rare red squirrels.

RESUPPLY NOTES:

There is absolutely nothing on this route except for Blair Atholl, Glenmore, Tomintoul, and Braemar, so use those for resupply. They make quite good markers for staging days. It's best to carry at least one meal's worth of food, just in case. Water is absolutely no problem in the Cairngorms. Take a water filter and be careful to drink straight from the rivers and streams.

ACCOMMODATIONS:

For the ultimate Cairngorms experience, wild camping and a night in a bothy should be on your list—just follow the "leave no trace" principles in these sensitive environments. Wild camping is permitted in Scotland. Hotels, hostels, bed-and-breakfasts, and campsites are options in Blair Atholl, Glenmore, Tomintoul, and Braemar.

GETTING THERE (AND BACK):

Blair Atholl is on the main train line and is a one-and-a-half-hour drive from both Edinburgh and Inverness.

RIDE SEASON:

Any time between April to October is possible but the shoulder seasons (April to June and September to October) are the best time to ride the Cairngorms Loop for the longer days, favorable weather, and fewer bugs. River crossings are a serious consideration on the Loop. Loaded bikes can be a good asset for crossing rivers, though—great to lean on—just avoid submerging moving parts with bearings, like wheel hubs and bottom brackets.

EQUIPMENT:

You'll need to be self-sufficient—bring shelter (camping kit) and some food supplies—and be prepared for any weather with emergency kit (first aid and survival blankets). While it is possible to do the Cairngorms Loop without camping, it leaves zero room for any setbacks.

WHAT TO RIDE:

You *could* ride the Outer Cairngorms Loop on anything from a gravel bike to a full-suspension mountain bike. On the Outer Loop, given the mix of trails, it is slower but comfier to be overbiked and somewhat fun and challenging to be underbiked. The Inner Loop is definitely mountain bike territory.

ROUTEMAKER:

The Cairngorms Loop is officially Steve Wilkinson's concept, evolving from the Tour of the Cairngorms route. Colin Cadden now helps with its stewardship and annual events.

CONTRIBUTOR INFO:

Stef Amato is a bikepacker based in the U.K.'s Peak District. As founder of Pannier, he curates, organizes, and hosts bikepacking experiences in the U.K. and further afield. Jordan Gibbons is a U.K.-based photojournalist. The pair have become good friends after many bikepacking trips together.

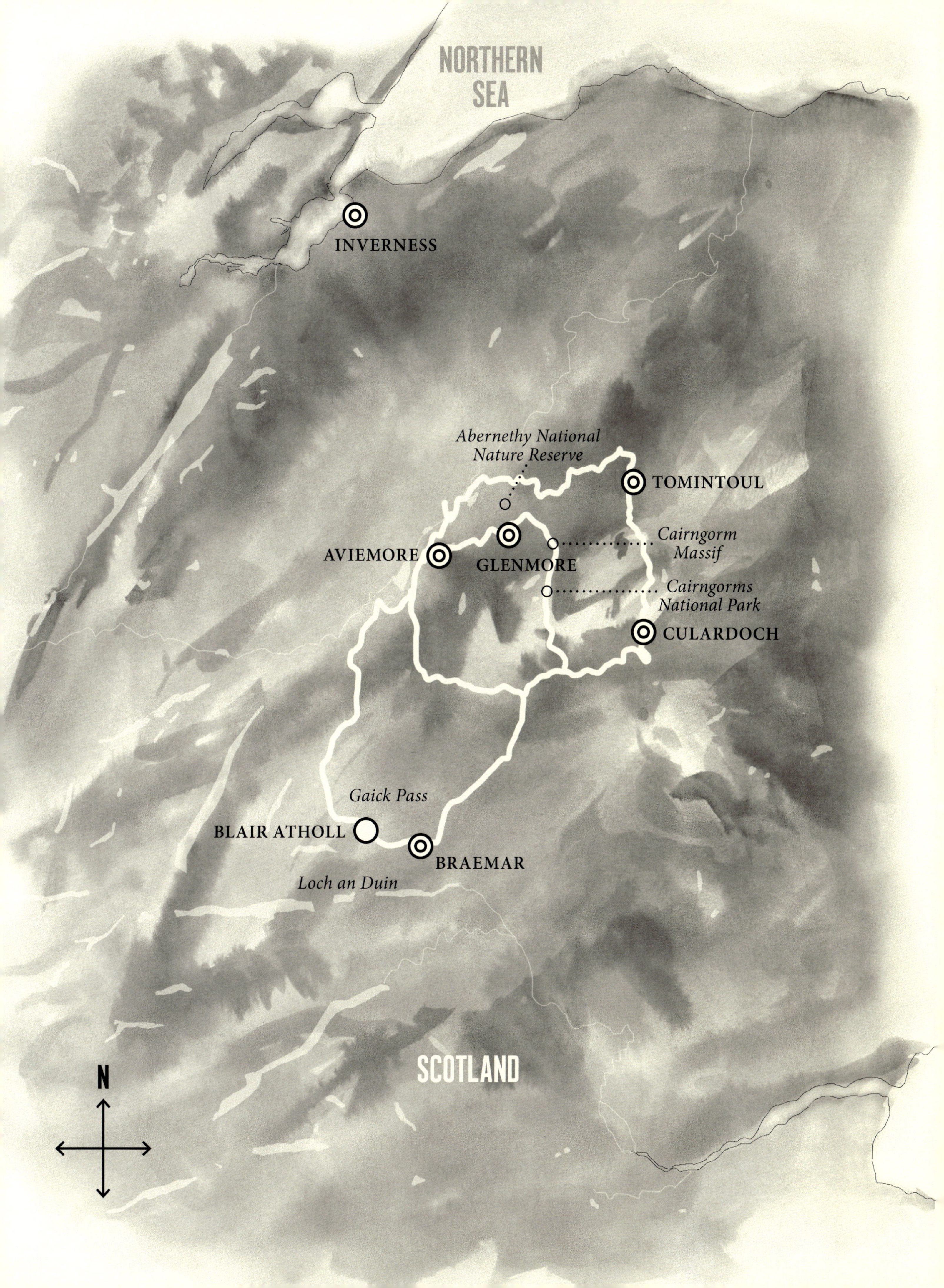

NORTHERN SEA
INVERNESS
Abernethy National Nature Reserve
TOMINTOUL
Cairngorm Massif
AVIEMORE
GLENMORE
Cairngorms National Park
CULARDOCH
Gaick Pass
BLAIR ATHOLL
BRAEMAR
Loch an Duin
SCOTLAND
N

SHELTER

The art of minimalism—balancing comfort, safety, and agility—comes with experience. Learning from your successes and mistakes is the best way to prepare for future adventures. These are the three main shelter options in the backcountry.

SEEKING A CAMP SPOT

- Flat and dry-ish
- Sheltered
- Away from roads, tracks, rockfall, animals, rivers, and steep drops
- Water supply for cooking, drinking, and washing bodies/sporks
- Pitch up just before dark to check surroundings and not attract attention

WILD CAMPING/LEAVE NO TRACE

- Research terrain and legalities
- Ask for permission
- Camp on durable surfaces
- Pack all trash out with you
- Cathole human waste
- Minimize campfire impact
- Respect animals and plants

BIVVY/TARP

Quick, simple, lightweight, but exposed. Tarps add fuss but provide additional shelter.

1 *Bivvy Bag*
2 *Tarp*
3 *Guylines*
4 *Stakes*
5 *Pole(s)*
6 *Sleeping mat*
7 *Sleeping bag/insulated jacket*
8 *Pillow*

TOP TIP: Leave your system together and roll up for a simple roll out in the evening.

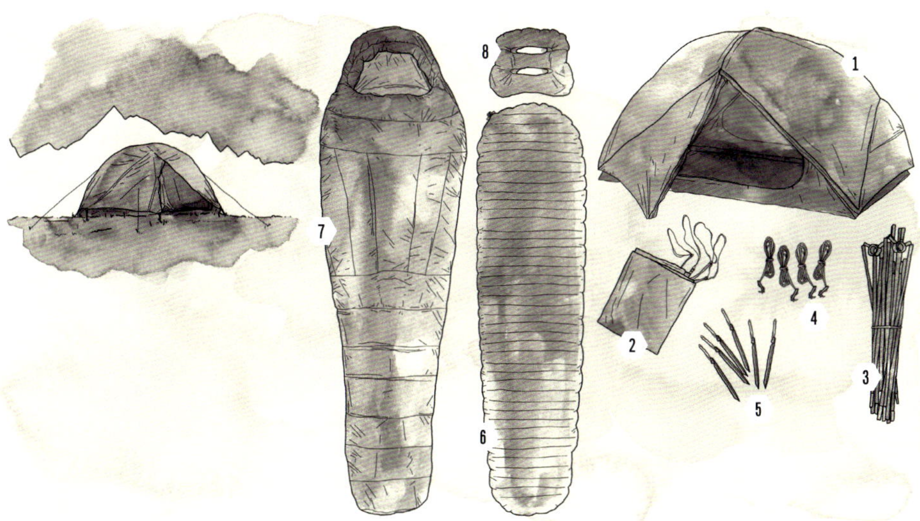

TENT

The go-to. Your home away from home.

1 *Tent inner/outer*
2 *Additional groundsheet*
3 *Poles*
4 *Guylines*
5 *Stakes*
6 *Sleeping mat*
7 *Sleeping bag*
8 *Pillow*

TOP TIP: Do not view a tent as a single item. Think about splitting up the various pieces to aid packability. (inner/outer in handlebar pack; poles/stakes in frame pack, etc.)

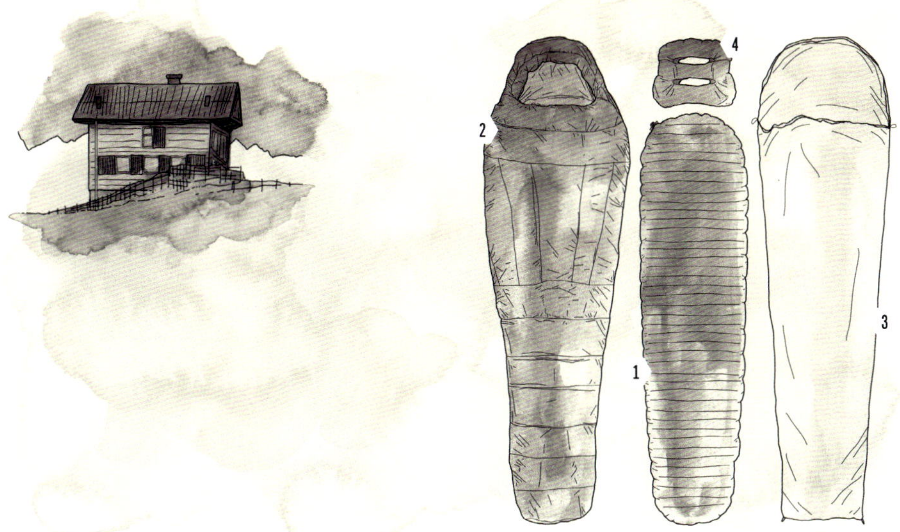

HUT

It offers less freedom than camping out, but the joy of reaching a pass-nesting mountain hut or remote stone bothy is unrivaled. Huts are a great introduction to bikepacking and mean carrying less kit.

1 *Sleeping mat*
2 *Sleeping bag*
3 *Sleeping bag liner*
4 *Pillow*

TOP TIP: Phone ahead to make sure the mountain huts are open and have space, and to give them a rough arrival time. Bring earplugs.

FOLLOW THE WHEEL TRACKS OF AN ORIGINAL BIKEPACKER

ROUTE:
ICELAND DIVIDE

LOCATION:
ICELAND

HORACE DALL WAS A MAN FAMILIAR with adventure. He had already made the first crossing of the High Atlas by bike—and ended up getting arrested by the French Foreign Legion and accused of being a spy. Despite his experience, he must have felt a degree of trepidation as he set off on an attempt to cross the Sprengisandur (the highland plateau of Iceland's interior) in 1933. He was armed with a Raleigh 3-speed roadster, a compass, a vague 1:1,000,000 map, a sleeping bag, and a stove. Fortunately, the pre-eminent optician also brought a camera and recorded his trip, writing notes on the back of some of his images. Those photos documented near impassable rivers and gorges, and soft sandy terrain that meant he was pushing his bike for 90 percent of the time. Despite those challenges, he became the first person to cross Iceland's interior on any form of wheeled transport. A local farmer was more than a little surprised to see a cyclist emerge from the wilderness, especially as Dall was immaculately dressed in a shirt, tie, and polished shoes. The farmer recalled it was as if he were going for a job interview in Reykjavík. Who says all bikepackers are dirtbags?

Much has changed in the intervening decades since Dall's groundbreaking journey. Gravel roads now link the north and south coasts of Iceland, and the route is well traversed each summer, but there are few places in the world that can instill such a sense of adventure. The classic direction for riding the route is the opposite of Horace. Riders now tend to start at the small city of Akureyri and make their way south to finish at Iceland's most southerly point at the town of Vík í Mýrdal.

The landscape quickly changes from vibrant greens surrounding Lake Svartárvatn to the monochromatic volcanic geology of the interior of the country as riders enter the most remote area of Iceland. Save for the odd yellow marker pole or signpost, the environment feels so lunar-like that it was used by NASA in the 1960s to prepare Apollo astronauts for the real thing. In the distance, tongues of glaciers stretch down to the moon-gray surface and volcanic mountain ranges frame the Sprengisandur plateau.

Huts dotted along the gravel roads offer weary travelers basic shelter from the incessant winds that rip across the plateau—moments of relative quiet and the opportunity to take stock as the weather roars outside. Many have a small heater and gas stove as well as a handful of sleeping platforms. The only problem is mustering up the motivation to leave these islands of comparative comfort and head back out into the wild.

Time does strange things this far north. The near 24 hours of daylight means that there is often no need to hurry—there's no darkness to beat. Yet the long gravel roads can feel →

"ONCE THE VOLCANIC DUST HAS BEEN WASHED OFF YOUR LEGS AND MEMORIES FADE OVER TIME, YOU CAN LOOK BACK ON A RIDE LIKE NO OTHER."

← LIGHTHOUSES TELL A TALE OF HARSH, REMOTE COASTLINES.
→ WILD CAMPING IS PERMITTED IN THE HIGHLANDS, BUT KEEP AN EYE ON THE WEATHER.
↓ A WET AND COLD WEATHER KIT IS A MUST-HAVE IN THE ICELANDIC HIGHLANDS.

GLACIAL AND WATER FEATURES LIKE ALDEYJARFOSS, AT THE NORTHERN PART OF THE SPRENGISANDUR ROAD, ARE A HIGHLIGHT OF THE ICELAND DIVIDE.

"THERE ARE FEW PLACES IN THE WORLD THAT CAN INSTILL SUCH A SENSE OF ADVENTURE."

HUTS DOT THE BLACK MOONSCAPE, OFFERING THE ONLY SHELTER AMONGST EXPOSED, WILD LANDS.

"THE NEAR 24-HOURS OF DAYLIGHT MEANS THAT THERE IS OFTEN NO NEED TO HURRY—THERE'S NO DARKNESS TO BEAT."

unending, especially if the wind blows from an unfavorable distance. Minutes feel like hours of churning through soft volcanic dust. But color makes its return in a spectacular manner, in the form of eye-popping green moss that somehow makes its home on the flanks of volcanoes. The rock takes on multicolored hues in the mountains of the Fjallabak Nature Reserve. And even the slowest of riders still make progress, eventually reaching the final doubletrack down to the southern coast.

There are many elements of Dall's crossing you won't want to emulate, but make sure there is one that you do: take photographs as you go to record the unbelievable scenery. Once the volcanic dust has been washed off your legs and memories fade over time, you can look back on a ride like no other. ○

CROSSING SEVERAL RIVERS A DAY, BIKEPACKING IN ICELAND MEANS GETTING USED TO WET FEET.

ICELAND'S WILD VOLCANIC INTERIOR IS A BIKEPACKING PLAYGROUND ADVENTURE LIKE NO OTHER.

ROUTE NOTES

Start: Akureyri, Iceland / **Finish:** Vík í Mýrdal, Iceland / **Distance:** 554 km (344 mi) / **Duration:** Approximately one week / **Category:** An epic adventure that defies the numbers / **Terrain:** Gravel roads / **Level:** Moderate

HIGHLIGHTS:

It is impossible to visit Iceland and not be wowed by the otherworldly landscape. There are too many standouts to list, but the route passes Goðafoss, one of the most impressive waterfalls in Iceland. Mount Mælifell is a majestic pyramid of a volcano that marks the exit from the Sprengisandur.

LOCAL SPECIALTIES:

Horace Dall brought just glucose and pemmican (dried meat mixed with fat and berries) to sustain him on his adventure. If you decide to replicate him, you'll be doubly keen to visit the Smiðjan Brugghús, a brewery taproom with great food, at the end of the route in Vík í Mýrdal.

WILDLIFE AND LANDSCAPE:

Expect to see little in the way of wildlife, but the incredible living geology of Iceland makes up for that: active volcanoes, basalt columns, solidified lava fields, and the lead-black sand on the beach at Vík, for starters.

RESUPPLY NOTES:

Water is in abundance and generally safe to drink from rivers, except near farms at the start/finish of the route. There are no food resupply options along the route so you'll need to bring all of your meals—dehydrated food is your friend here. It is small and light and just needs warm water to "cook."

ACCOMMODATIONS:

There are some free-to-use huts along the route, but they should not be solely relied upon: they may be booked up or full, or conditions may mean your progress is slower than expected. We suggest you don't take a leaf out of Dall's book and just bring a sleeping bag. A tent will be a welcome shelter from the wind and elements.

GETTING THERE (AND BACK):

Fly to Reykjavík. Both ends of the route are accessible by public bus. Icelandic buses are equipped with bike racks.

RIDE SEASON:

The access roads across Iceland's interior are closed for most of the year due to snow. It's only really possible to ride the route from the beginning of June to the end of August.

EQUIPMENT:

Tent, stove, and food for your planned duration. Cold/wet weather clothing.

WHAT TO RIDE:

While the route is largely on gravel roads, the gravel can be deep and soft. For that reason, many people use fat bikes or similar high-volume tires to "float" over the terrain. A gravel bike will still be fine, but you may end up walking a little more.

OTHER IMPORTANT INFORMATION:

Don't be fooled into thinking this is an easy route. The weather and challenges that river crossings bring make the route a more serious proposition than the statistics suggest. River crossings can be dangerous after rain or even warm weather (in the case of glacial meltwater). You may need to wait for late night or early morning to make some crossings of glacial rivers.

ROUTEMAKER:

While Horace Dall made the first crossing, he was given a lift in a boat across one of the rivers in the south. Dick Phillips made the first unassisted crossing in 1958. Even then, he had to bring a dinghy and rope for some of the river crossings.

CONTRIBUTOR INFO:

Joffrey Maluski is a French traveler and photographer based in South East of France. His work mainly focuses on the outdoor adventures and landscapes.

N
NORWEGIAN SEA
AKUREYRI
Goðafoss
Svartárvatn
ICELAND
Sprengisandur
REYKJAVÍK
Mælifell
Fjallabak
Nature Reserve
VÍK Í MÝRDAL
ATLANTIC OCEAN

TRAILSIDE FIXES

Adventuring off-road in remote places by bike is tough on both bikepackers and equipment, not only because of challenging terrain but also the increased loads and harsh conditions. Here are the key kits, tools, spares, and fixes to know and carry to keep you and your bike on track.

CHECKLIST OF COMMON FIXES

While it is easy to ignore the fact that things might go wrong, the side of a remote track in a storm is not the best place to start learning how to fix the basics. Before you leave, have a mechanic check your bike over.

The most likely parts to need maintenance during a bikepacking adventure will be those that are used the most, vulnerable, or with moving parts. With the exception of a few major failures or breaks that require more specific tools and knowledge—such as hubs and hydraulics—most issues are fixable with a few basics that you should carry.

A *Fixing a Flat Tire—Tube/Tubeless*
1 / 3 / 4 / 6 / 14 / 17 / 22
B *Repairing a Split Tire*
1 / 3 / 5 / 16 / 32
C *Installing/Removing Pedals*
2
D *Adjusting Brakes/Replacing Brake Pads*
2 / 11 / 23
E *Adjusting Gears—Cable Tensions/Derailleur Alignments*
2 / 11
F *Fixing/Replacing a Chain*
7 / 10 / 11 / 18 / 19
G *Adjusting Handlebars/Stems/Headsets/Saddle/Seatpost*
2
H *Replacing Cables*
2 / 11 / 12 / 27

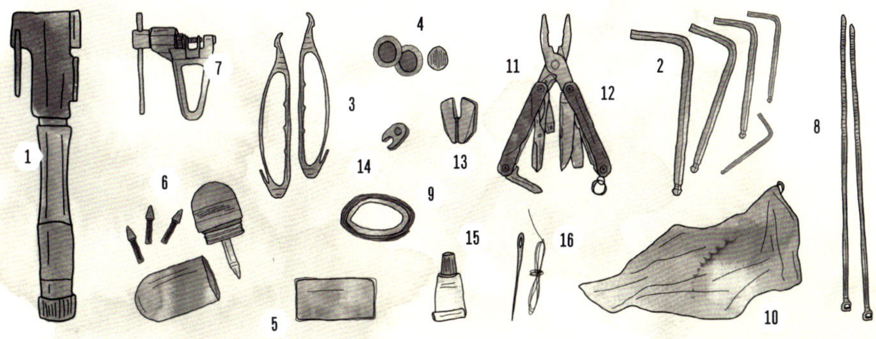

TOOLS GRID

ESSENTIAL: 1 ***Pump.*** 2 ***Allen/hex keys.*** 3 ***Tire levers.*** 4 ***Patch kit.*** 5 ***Tire boot.*** 6 ***Tubeless plugs kit.*** 7 ***Chain breaker.*** 8 ***Zip ties.*** 9 ***Duct/electrical tape.*** 10 ***Rag.*** 11 ***Pliers.*** 12 ***Cutters.*** *EXPEDITION:* 13 ***Spoke key.*** 14 ***Valve extractor.*** 15 ***Super glue.*** 16 ***Needle and thread.*** Multi-tools have various separate tools like chain breakers, tubeless plugs, and pliers integrated on them, so check how you can efficiently carry less.

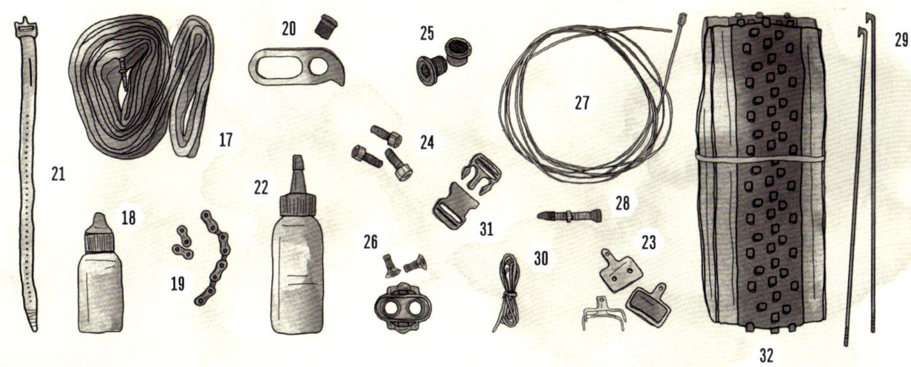

SPARES GRID

ESSENTIAL: 17 ***Inner tubes (check sizing).*** 18 ***Chain lube.*** 19 ***Chain section and quick links (check compatibility).*** 20 ***Derailleur/mech hanger (check compatibility).*** 21 ***Bungee/strap.*** *EXPEDITION:* 22 ***30–50 ml tubeless sealant.*** 23 ***Brake pads (check compatibility).*** 24 ***Bolts (M4/M5).*** 25 ***Chain-ring nuts and bolts.*** 26 ***Cleat and cleat bolts.*** 27 ***Brake/gear cables.*** 28 ***Valves.*** 29 ***Spokes (check lengths).*** 30 ***Guyline/lace.*** 31 ***Bag buckles.*** 32 ***Tire.***

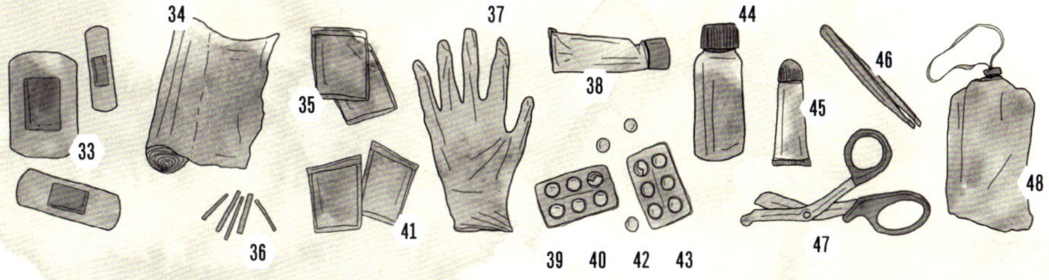

FIRST AID GRID

33 ***Adhesive bandages.*** 34 ***Bandage dressings.*** 35 ***Sterile wipes.*** 36 ***Steristrips.*** 37 ***Rubber gloves.*** 38 ***Hydrocortisone/ Sudocrem (for saddle sores).*** 39 ***Painkillers.*** 40 ***Antibiotics.*** 41 ***Dioralyte electrolyte sachets (for rehydration).*** 42 ***Diamox (for altitude).*** 43 ***Antihistamines (for allergies).*** 44 ***TCP antiseptic liquid.*** 45 ***Lip balm.*** 46 ***Tweezers/tick pullers.*** 47 ***Small scissors.*** 48 ***Emergency bivvy.***

SINGLETRACK STOKE THROUGH BACKCOUNTRY OREGON

ROUTE:
OREGON TIMBER TRAIL

LOCATION:
UNITED STATES

PICK ANY ROUTE from this book—or almost any bikepacking route in the world—and it is likely that the majority of the route will be on roads, tracks, and trails that have been in existence long before the route itself. And for the most part that infrastructure wasn't designed with riding in mind—it just so happens that a bicycle is a great tool for exploration.

So there is something novel, and joyful, about riding a trail that has been specifically designed and built with cyclists in mind; whether that's a great inner-city segregated bike path or a mountain bike flow trail in the woods. The Oregon Timber Trail stands out in this regard. It was only created in 2017 and was specifically designed and constructed with mountain biking in mind. The Oregon Timber Trail Alliance (OTTA) has taken a proactive approach to trail development, logging (no pun intended) over 10,000 hours of volunteer work to restore previously neglected trails, further enhance other existing trails, and construct tracts of new singletrack to link everything together. In doing so, the OTTA established its legacy as a trail stewardship leader, folding in elements of education, history, and community engagement alongside the physical building and maintenance of the route.

Starting at the Californian border in the south, the route trends northwards through Oregon to the Washington border. Along the way, the trail is split into four "tiers" or legs: the Fremont Tier, Willamette Tier, Deschutes Tier, and Hood Tier, each with their own unique feel, landscape, and ecosystems. Linking them together is an epic undertaking, not just because of the distance but because the trails have been built as technically challenging and engaging singletrack.

The route begins with possibly the most challenging tier and starts, aptly, in "the middle of nowhere," according to the OTTA. Fourteen thousand years ago, much of the low basin range country and alkali lakes of the area were part of a giant inland sea teeming with wildlife that provided food for North America's first settlers. Today the sea has dried up but trout streams, bird life, and even some relaxing hot springs punctuate the land left behind.

Dry deserts, sparse ponderosa forests, and wide-open rangeland give way to dark, verdant, and loamy forests as soon as you crest the Cascades and ride through the Willamette Tier. The Deschutes Tier then takes riders over the volcanic eastern flank of the Cascade Range; your tires won't touch tarmac once over its 182-kilometer (113-mile) length. Bend is famous for its large network of world-class mountain bike trails and the Oregon Timber Trail takes full advantage of them as it passes through.

Riders heading into the Hood Tier may think they're on the final →

“THERE IS SOMETHING NOVEL, AND JOYFUL, ABOUT RIDING A TRAIL THAT HAS BEEN SPECIFICALLY DESIGNED AND BUILT WITH CYCLISTS IN MIND.”

← THERE IS AN ANNUAL MASS-START OF THE OTT. BIKEPACKING TRIPS ARE BEST SHARED.
→ YOU'LL FIND ADVENTURE ON THIS 1,070-KILOMETER (670-MILE) OFF-ROAD ROUTE.
↓ THE OTT MAKES USE OF EXISTING WORLD-CLASS MOUNTAIN BIKE TRAILS.

HISTORICALLY, TRAILS ARE THE OLDEST FORM OF COMMUNICATION, AND BEST WAY FOR ENABLING COMMUNITIES TO FORM. THE OTTA IS A GREAT EXAMPLE.

"IT IS HARD TO IMAGINE A TRAIL THAT COULD PACK IN MORE IN THAT DISTANCE."

stretch—if they haven't looked at the elevation profile. Countless backcountry ridges and streams tease you with imposing views of Mount Jefferson and Mount Hood itself. The Olallie Lake Scenic Area is a quiet, high-elevation landscape speckled with pristine pocket lakes brimming with trout (and mosquitos), and wonderful campsites abound. The final descent of the route sums up everything that is great about this true mountain bikers' route. The rowdy and rapid trail down to Columbia River Gorge spits you out at the trail end with little else to do other than dip your tires and toes in the Columbia River.

The Oregon Timber Trail is shorter than many of the routes featured in this book, yet it is hard to imagine a trail that could pack in more in that distance. That it exists at all is testament to the ambitions and efforts of the OTTA. The result is a route that sits as one of the greatest long-distance mountain bike routes in the world. ○

ROUTE NOTES

Start: 32 km (20 mi) south of Lakeview, Oregon, USA / **Finish:** Hood River, Oregon, USA / **Distance:** 1,077 km (669 mi) / **Duration:** 20–30 days / **Category:** Multi-week point-to-point / **Terrain:** Almost entirely unpaved, with 80 % singletrack riding / **Level:** Difficult

HIGHLIGHTS:

Each tier of the trail has its own highlights, whether you are riding for the views, landscape, and wildlife or get your kicks from the singletrack itself.

LOCAL SPECIALTIES:

Oakridge is a sleepy little logging town but one of the larger on the route. It's well worth visiting the brewery or distillery and digging into a large BBQ.

WILDLIFE AND LANDSCAPE:

Watch out for raccoons, squirrels, and other scavengers that may chew their way into your food stash. There's a chance you'll bump into a black bear or mountain lion, but they prefer to leave you alone.

RESUPPLY NOTES:

There are few towns to find resupply in and often a single convenience store from which to stock up. There are some sections of trail with very limited water source options. Make sure you can carry 4–5 liters of water for dry sections.

ACCOMMODATIONS:

Camping is available along the route. There are lots of national forest campsites with varying amenities, and unless expressly forbidden, wild camping is allowed.

GETTING THERE (AND BACK):

The start is difficult to access via public transport, but the easiest option is probably taking an Amtrak train from Portland, Oregon, to Klamath Falls, Oregon. From there, it is a 165 km (100 mi) ride to Lakeview, or there is an alternative start option from Klamath Falls itself that links into the trail at the 110 km (70 mi) mark. Hood River is around 96 km (60 mi.) from Portland.

RIDE SEASON:

Late June to mid-October. High-elevation snowpack usually melts enough to be passable by mid-June. Expect overnight temperatures around freezing all year round on high sections.

EQUIPMENT:

In addition to standard bikepacking and camping gear, a water filter and head net (early season) are strongly recommended.

WHAT TO RIDE:

A mountain bike. Suspension—front, rear, or both—will make the going more comfortable.

OTHER IMPORTANT INFORMATION:

Forest fires can be a real issue and cause parts of the trail to be closed or diverted. Keep an eye on official websites for live updates.

HISTORY:

The route first opened in 2015.

CONTRIBUTOR INFO:

Conan Thai is a photographer based in New York City, USA, and always available for adventures.

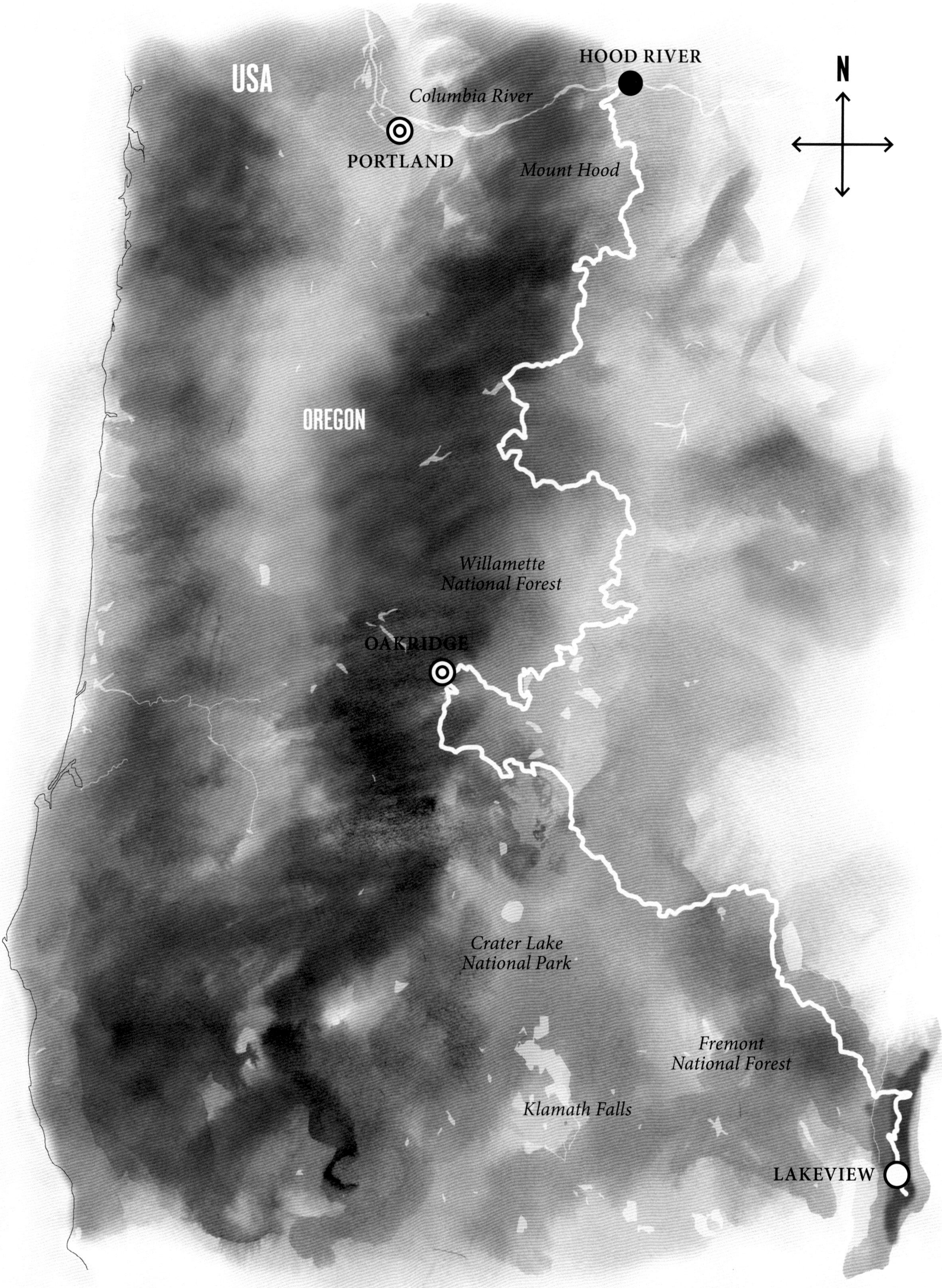
HOOD RIVER
USA
N
Columbia River
PORTLAND
Mount Hood
OREGON
Willamette
National Forest
OAKRIDGE
Crater Lake
National Park
Fremont
National Forest
Klamath Falls
LAKEVIEW

ALTITUDE AND ATTITUDE ON THE ROOF OF THE ROCKIES

ROUTE:
COLORADO TRAIL

LOCATION:
UNITED STATES

↑ NOW 30 YEARS OLD, THIS CLASSIC NORTH AMERICAN ROUTE IS MAINTAINED BY THE COLORADO TRAIL FOUNDATION.
→ CT SINGLETRACK WEAVES THROUGH THE ROCKY MOUNTAINS AT A 3,000-METER (10,000-FOOT) AVERAGE ABOVE SEA LEVEL, MAKING FOR A CHALLENGING ADVENTURE.

IF YOU ARE LOOKING FOR THE ULTIMATE bikepacking test—one that requires the rider to possess fitness, technical bike-handling skills, and high-altitude endurance—then few routes fit the bill better than the Colorado Trail (CT). The pay-off for that physical exertion is what the Colorado Trail Foundation describes as “mile for mile, the most beautiful trail in America.” That might be reason enough, but throw in endless flowing singletrack and engaging descents, and most mountain bikers are left chomping at the bit. There is good reason that the CT is considered one of the all-time classic bikepacking routes.

The trail starts in Denver and travels in a broadly southwest direction to Durango, traversing the Rocky Mountains and crossing the U.S. Continental Divide. In doing so, it passes through rich alpine scenery. Think meadows bursting with wildflowers, bleak and arid rocky ridges, and shady aspen forests. The CT isn’t a pure wilderness expedition though. It also visits historic mountain towns, many set up in the mining boom of the late 1800s (no prizes for guessing what was mined around Silverton, but strangely silver was also Leadville’s main resource). Depending on your pace, they make for perfect stopovers or speedy pit-stops and a break from the relentless nature of the trail itself.

Our minds are good at blanking out pain—those moments on the trail when we swear we’ll never get on a bike again, curse the weather or our own weaknesses, and question our choices. Instead, we treasure the memories of heart-stopping views or heart-racing descents. Every retelling of the Colorado Trail includes those golden moments: the long ripsnorting singletrack descent from Ten Mile Pass to Copper Mountain, which splinters into steep rock gardens requiring skill and care to negotiate; the swooping trail around Twin Lakes that makes it impossible not to let out a “whoop!” as you rail around; perfect picnic spots; dips in snowmelt lakes. Dig a little deeper with a CT veteran though, and you begin to discover a little more about how tough the Colorado Trail truly is.

The 3,000-meter (10,000-foot) average altitude is enough to bring even the fittest riders to their knees. It’s generally recommended to complete the route from north to →

south, as it gives you a slightly more gradual acclimatization, but even then your lungs are likely to complain right out of the block. Easy gradients can feel like riding through molasses while breathing through a straw. Steeper pitches quickly become a walk. Technical climbs require the bike to be shouldered and carried, step by slow step. It is moments like these when the bike itself becomes an impediment to progress; an anchor that is merely tolerated on the promise of delivering fun a few miles further along the trail. There is, though, a strange and almost reassuringly monotonous pattern to this plodding, despite the ever-changing backdrop—progress is progress, even if it is achingly slow. But add into the mix unpredictable weather—high daytime temperatures, violent afternoon thunderstorms, freak snow flurries, and freezing overnight camps that take their toll on already tired bodies—and you begin to realize why it is estimated

that only 30 percent who start the Colorado Trail complete it.

And maybe that's what makes the CT such a classic; it isn't great despite the hardships it presents, it is great because it is so hard. Every glorious moment along its 913 kilometers (567 miles) is bought and paid for with hard work. Lung-ripping, leg-wilting hard work with no guarantee of success. Somehow, the Colorado Trail has found the magic recipe that combines the stuff of nightmares and dreams in one package and is oh-so-much richer as a result. ○

MOST BIKEPACKERS TAKE AROUND TWO WEEKS TO RIDE THE 1,000-KILOMETER (620-MILE) TRAIL BETWEEN DENVER AND DURANGO. THE RECORD IS JUST OVER FOUR DAYS.

ROUTE NOTES

Start: Denver, Colorado, USA / **Finish:** Durango, Colorado, USA / **Distance:** 913 km (567 mi) / **Duration:** 4–14 days / **Category:** Epic multiday adventure, point-to-point / **Terrain:** 80 % off-road, a large proportion of which is singletrack / **Level:** Difficult

HIGHLIGHTS:

The trails from Ten Mile Pass and around Twin Lakes are frequently listed as some of the best singletrack descending on the route. The stretch from Silverton to Durango offers spectacular views and another incredible descent into town if you are still fresh enough to enjoy it.

LOCAL SPECIALTIES:

If you are really lucky you might bump into one of the "trail angels" who cook up homemade food for thru-hikers and riders. Many towns have their own breweries, if you fancy taking a relaxed approach to rehydration and don't have too far to travel to sleep that evening.

WILDLIFE AND LANDSCAPE:

Bears are commonly sighted along the trail, so take appropriate precautions. Wildflowers speckle the high meadows in early season, and the aspen trees begin their transition into fall shades in September.

RESUPPLY NOTES:

There are a number of towns along, or just off, the route but depending on your pace, there may be multiday stretches without resupply. Breckenridge, Leadville, Buena Vista, and Silverton are popular stops to restock. Water is usually readily available along the route; bring a water filter and carrying capacity for a couple of liters and make use of creeks and springs when you pass.

ACCOMMODATIONS:

Many of the towns have hostels, hotels, and motels, but you will need to bring camping kit for the more remote sections. There are both wild camping and campsite options along the route.

GETTING THERE (AND BACK):

There is no formal shuttle service between Denver and Durango. Both cities are served by an airport.

RIDE SEASON:

Snow makes many of the high passes unnavigable until early July each year, and returns by September, leaving a short ride season. Even then, expect some lingering snow during July, and volatile mountain weather throughout the summer. In general, aim to have cleared high passes by mid-afternoon to avoid the risk of being exposed during a thunderstorm.

EQUIPMENT:

There is a real balance to be had on the Colorado Trail; bring enough gear and clothing to stay safe in the high alpine terrain, but travel minimally enough to make climbing and hike-a-bike sections bearable. Ensure your luggage has enough space to carry several days' worth of food. The trail is signposted, but you'll want some form of additional navigation.

WHAT TO RIDE:

The CT is mountain bike terrain, and it can be rocky and demanding in places. A short-travel full-suspension bike is probably ideal, but a hardtail with wide tires is also sufficient.

OTHER IMPORTANT INFORMATION:

The route has an average altitude of over 3,000 m (10,000 ft) and reaches as high as 4,000 m (13,000 ft). If traveling from sea level, it is worth giving yourself some time to acclimatize before starting the route, and/or adjusting your pace expectations to take into account the thin air. The mountain bike route does not follow the Colorado Trail exactly, as riding is forbidden in several wilderness areas. Ensure you follow the designated riding route.

HISTORY:

The route was created primarily as a thru-hiking trail in 1974, but it took until 1987 to fully build it. It is maintained by the Colorado Trail Foundation.

CONTRIBUTOR INFO:

Michael Dammer and his family are riding bikes, exploring high mountains and making a living on a sustainable organic farm in Ecuador.

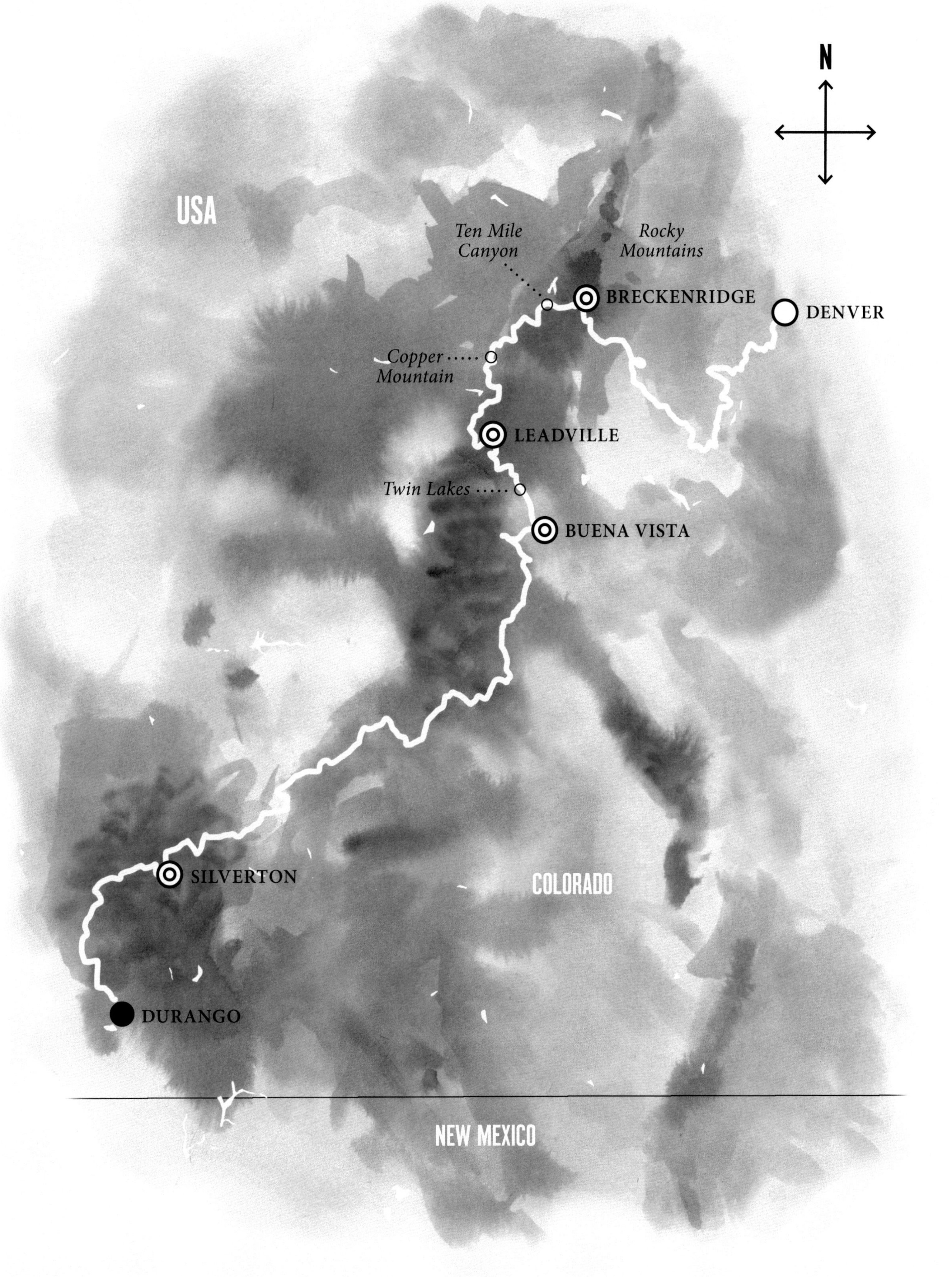
N
USA
Ten Mile Canyon
Rocky Mountains
BRECKENRIDGE
DENVER
Copper Mountain
LEADVILLE
Twin Lakes
BUENA VISTA
SILVERTON
COLORADO
DURANGO
NEW MEXICO

RIDE THE LENGTH OF AMERICA IN ICONIC STYLE

ROUTE:
GREAT DIVIDE MOUNTAIN BIKE ROUTE

LOCATION:
CANADA AND UNITED STATES

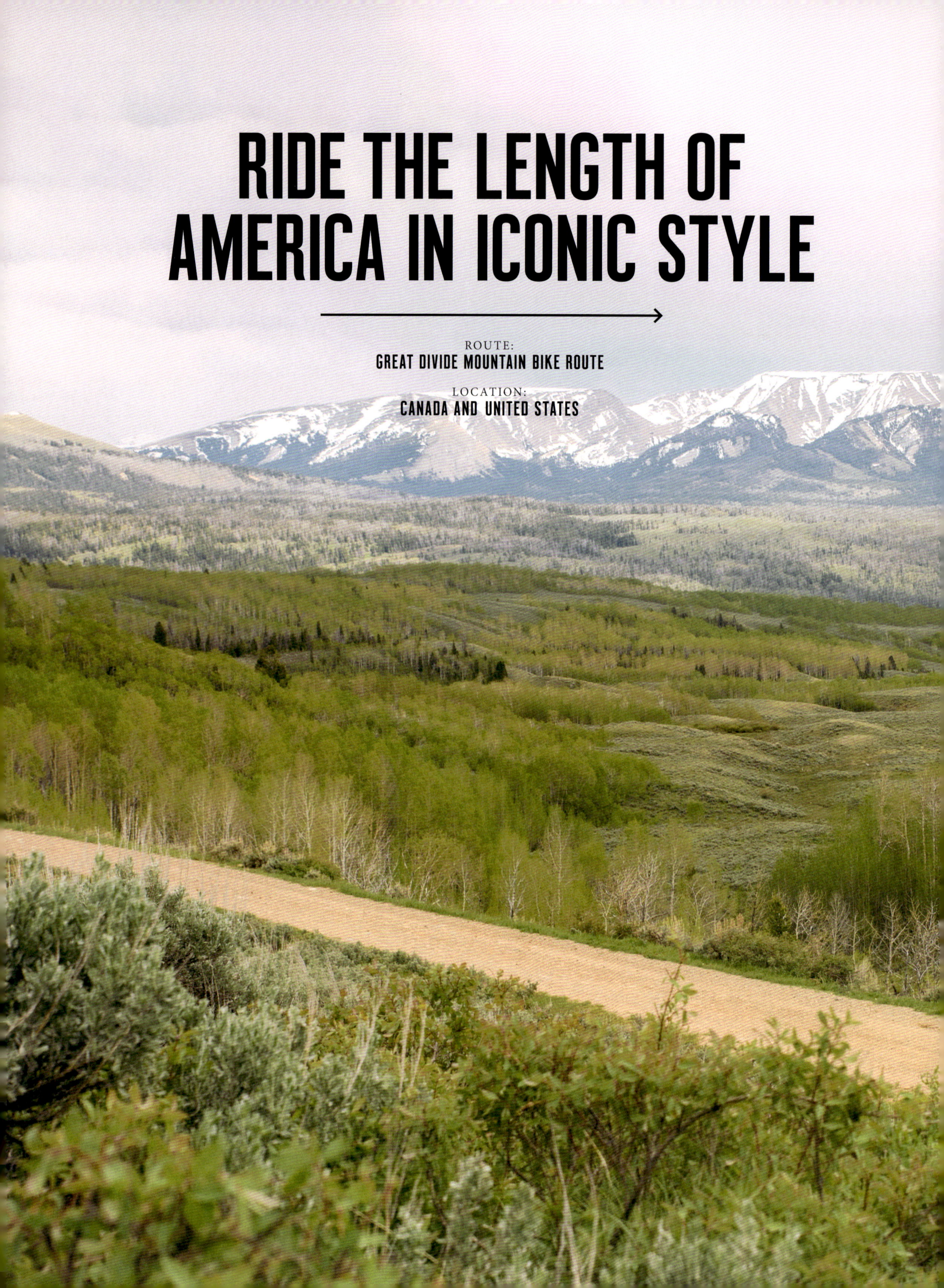

THE "DIVIDE" IS ARGUABLY THE ROUTE that gave birth to modern bikepacking. Its influence touches almost every aspect of the lightweight touring game as we now understand it; from the boom in popularity, to the evolution of gear, and the self-supported racing ethos. In fact, there are times when it is hard to separate the history of the route from the history of bikepacking, so wide has been its reach.

The Great Divide Mountain Bike Route (GDMBR)—to give it its full name—was first developed by Michael McCoy of the Adventure Cycling Association in 1997, following a line tracing the watershed of America: the Continental Divide. The route actually begins in Banff, Canada, before crossing the U.S. border and finally terminating at the U.S.-Mexican border in Antelope Wells, New Mexico, 4,418 kilometers (2,745 miles) later. Following the traditional north-south direction, riders pass through national parks, wilderness areas,

high-altitude landscapes, and dusty deserts. Many experience snowy passes in Canada and Montana and searing heat in the Chihuahuan Desert. The route hopscotches between towns, providing resupply in roadside diners with stereotypically generous American portion sizes, before retreating to quiet backcountry.

The first recorded attempt at a "Fastest Known Time" (FKT) along the route was by the legendary John Stamstad in 1999. A few years later Mike Curiak took on the challenge, and 12 months later, in 2004, decided to organize a mass-start event along the U.S. section of the route: the now defunct Great Divide Race (GDR). →

THE ICONIC GREAT DIVIDE CONNECTS OVER 4,000 KILOMETERS (2,485 MILES) OF THE FINEST OFF-ROAD DIRT AND GRAVEL ROUTES THROUGH NORTH AMERICA.

CURATOR MICHAEL (MAC) MCCOY SCOUTED AND STITCHED THE ROUTE TOGETHER THROUGH THE 1990S, AIMING TO STAY AS CLOSE TO THE CONTINENTAL DIVIDE AS POSSIBLE WHILST THINKING ABOUT RESUPPLY TOWNS AND RESOURCES ALONG THE WAY.

"THE PAY-OFF, IF YOU ASK ANYONE WHO HAS COMPLETED IT, IS A LIFE-CHANGING EXPERIENCE."

One of the seven starters that year was Matthew Lee. In 2007, he launched the Tour Divide race, extending the route to take in the Canadian section of the GDMBR. It is this race that has endured and is now a mainstay in the competitive bikepacking calendar.

While the route is no doubt iconic in its own right, the Tour Divide race raised its profile even further. To many, it is the bikepacking race and more than that, it (and the GDR before it) has acted as a template for bikepacking racing the world over. The loose set of guidelines first developed for GDR evolved into the self-supported rules that are applied to the vast majority of current races. It is nonstop, and riders must be wholly responsible for their own self-sufficiency, with no outside help from either the organizers or a support crew.

Record times on the Tour Divide have been nibbled away over the years, with the current FKT of 13 days, 22 hours, and 51 minutes set by Mike Hall in 2016. Lael Wilcox holds the fastest female time of 15 days, 10 hours, and 59 minutes, set in 2015. If riding the route in one direction all sounds a little too easy, Billy Rice set the record for the "yo-yo" in 2013 when he rode the route northbound, then south, in one go, in a total time of 44 days and 42 minutes.

The Tour Divide (and a handful of other emerging races) were a fundamental cog in the development and innovation of bikepacking luggage, as riders sought to minimize weight, →

THE GREAT DIVIDE IS THE ORIGINAL "DIVIDE" ROUTE, AND NO DOUBT AT THE TOP OF EVERY BIKEPACKER'S BUCKET LIST.

streamline their gear, and improve reliability over the rough terrain. Framebags, saddlepacks, and bar rolls were significantly lighter and less cumbersome than a rack and panniers. As a result, some of the early cottage-industry manufacturers like Revelate Designs grew to become some of the most recognizable names in bikepacking as more and more riders, from would-be racers to leisure riders all around the globe began to see the benefits of a lighter-weight approach.

Storytelling has always gone hand in hand with the GDMBR, creating an even greater aura around the route. McCoy documented his early trips in the Adventure Cycling Association magazine and there have been countless books and articles written about the route since. The feature-length documentary *Ride the Divide* followed racers along its length in 2009, sharing their highs and lows, attrition and endurance, and perhaps brought the route to its largest audience thus far.

Despite the inevitable interest in the annual race, far more people tour along the route than take the start line, perhaps inspired by the daring trail tales and stoked to experience the adventure for themselves. Given its length, the GDMBR is a once-in-a-lifetime ride for many—the kind of ride that takes years of preparation and additional leave from the everyday routine just to contemplate setting off. The pay-off, if you ask anyone who has completed it, is a life-changing experience. The combination of immense physical challenge and epic landscapes leaves its mark on the individual, just as the GDMBR has left its own indelible influence on cycling culture. ○

ROUTE NOTES

Start: Banff, Canada / **Finish:** Antelope Wells, New Mexico, USA / **Distance:** 4,418 km (2,745 mi) / **Duration:** 3–6 weeks / **Category:** Multi-week transcontinental journey / **Terrain:** 90 % off-road, with most riding on dirt and gravel roads / **Level:** Moderate

HIGHLIGHTS:

Everyone who has ridden the entire length of the route will have their own personal highlights; one thing that makes the route so special is the diversity and contrast over the distance. Standouts include the Indiana Pass in Colorado (the route's highest point at 3,630 m / 11,913 ft); the alpine terrain of the Grand Teton National Park; the wide-open Great Divide Basin in Wyoming; the sunbaked Chihuahuan Desert; and the otherworldly finish line in Antelope Wells, New Mexico.

LOCAL SPECIALTIES:

Cross your fingers that you reach Pie Town, New Mexico on a day that the Toaster House is open. You know what to order …

WILDLIFE AND LANDSCAPE:

Expect to experience every type of landscape over the course of the route. Be aware of bears and mountain lions in the northern part of the route. Less dangerous wildlife includes eagles, deer, and elk. You will likely encounter mosquitos.

RESUPPLY NOTES:

The route regularly passes through towns and villages, but there are gaps of up to 170 km (106 mi) between resupply points. Study the route in detail and plan accordingly. Make the most of the hearty portions served in American eateries.

ACCOMMODATIONS:

Due to the length of some of the stretches between towns, some form of camp setup will be required. There are plenty of hotels and motels along the route though, perfect for charging electronics and grabbing the odd shower.

GETTING THERE (AND BACK):

Calgary is the nearest airport to Banff. El Paso (Texas) and Tucson (Arizona) are the nearest airports to the finish. The Adventure Cycling Association has a list of shuttle services that can ferry you to the start and finish of the route if you'd rather not turn a pedal for one more stroke than necessary.

RIDE SEASON:

North-south riders usually set off no earlier than late June. There is still a good chance you will find snow on high sections in the north, but they are likely to be passable. Study current conditions before setting off, but passes will likely be clear before June. The route has had to be diverted as a result of forest fires in recent years. Obey any signs, and check the Adventure Cycling Association website for current conditions. The route is normally passable until mid-October.

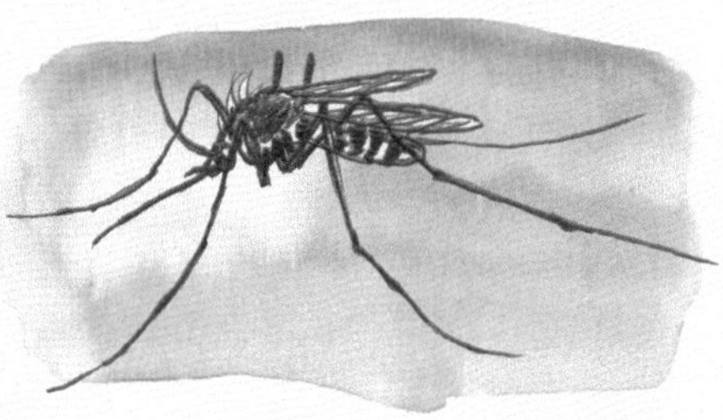

EQUIPMENT:

Little in the way of specialist equipment is needed, beyond standard bikepacking gear. Be prepared for extremes of weather along the route, ensure you have sufficient water/food carrying capacity on your bike, and bring some method of water filtration. Bring a mosquito net and bear spray.

WHAT TO RIDE:

Despite the high proportion of dirt roads, most riders use a lightweight mountain bike. This is largely for comfort over long sections of washboard terrain. While countless riders complete the route on a fully rigid bike, a modicum of suspension will be welcomed by most. Wide tires guard against punctures and also contribute toward comfort.

OTHER IMPORTANT INFORMATION:

As well as carrying bear spray, follow safe practice when camping, especially when it comes to food.

ROUTEMAKER:

Michael McCoy and the Adventure Cycling Association originally devised the route.

CONTRIBUTOR INFO:

Spencer Harding is a bike traveler and photographer based in Arizona, USA. He enjoys strapping camping gear to his bike and getting lost in the mountains.

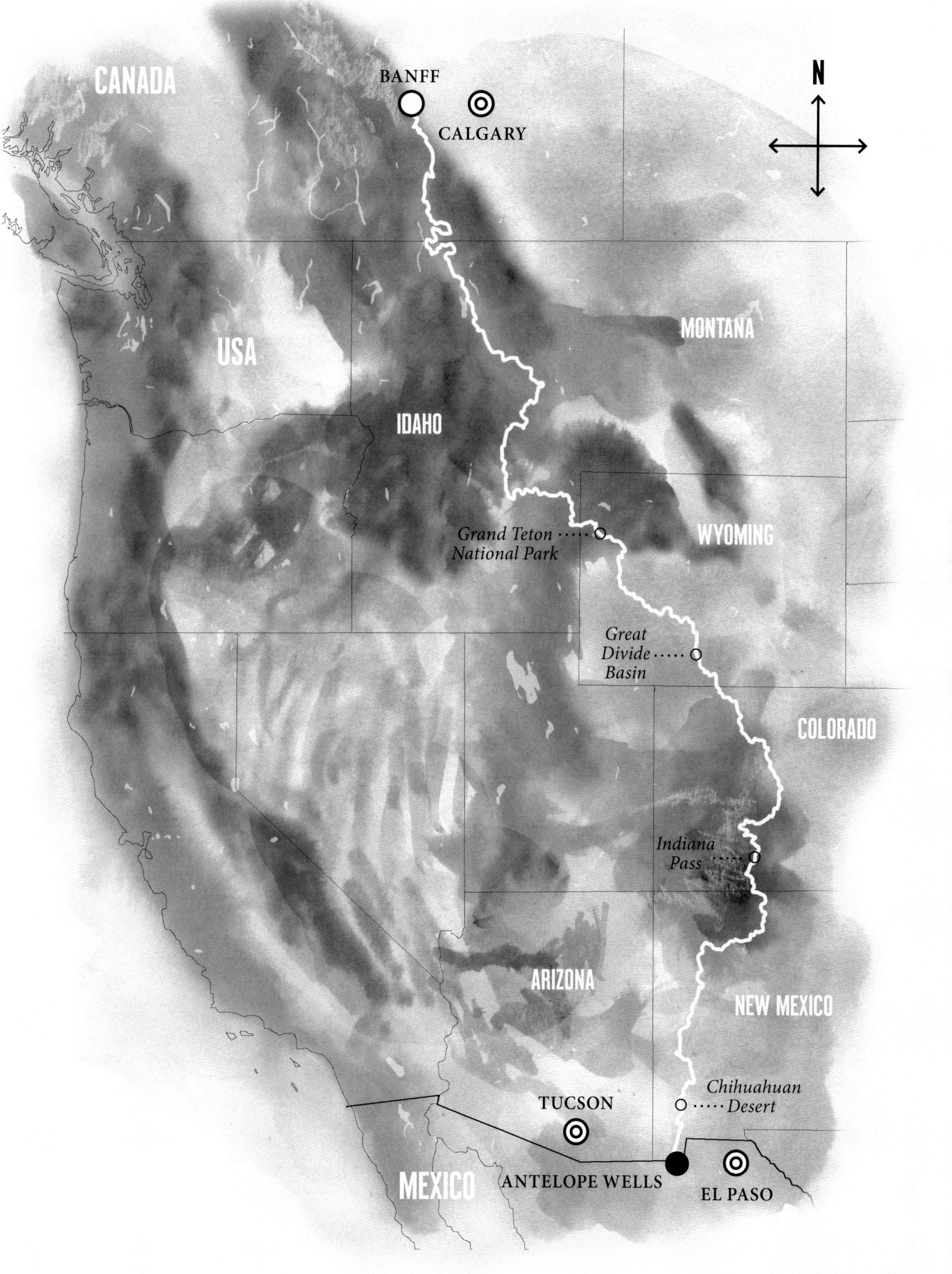

CANADA
BANFF
CALGARY
N
USA
MONTANA
IDAHO
Grand Teton
National Park
WYOMING
Great
Divide
Basin
COLORADO
Indiana
Pass
ARIZONA
NEW MEXICO
Chihuahuan
Desert
TUCSON
MEXICO
ANTELOPE WELLS
EL PASO

COPING WITH EXTREMES

Many of the routes featured in this book bring their own specific challenges that go beyond riding your bike a long way. Climate, landscape, and altitude all play their part. They can shape the distance you can cover each day, the physical impact on your body (and what you need to do to manage that), and the kit you need to bring. Take the time to research what you are likely to encounter on your route, and be prepared for the worst (while hoping for the best).

HEAT

In many ways, high temperatures are the most difficult to deal with on a bike. You can always add another layer in the cold, but there is no escaping the heat. Having said that, there are plenty of tricks you can apply that will make the experience easier to deal with.

- There's a reason that desert natives usually wear loose-fitting clothing. It helps create air circulation and aids cooling. Long sleeves might seem counterintuitive, but help prevent sunburn.
- Water is fundamental. Dehydration is a killer and accelerates heat stroke. Study your route and find out how frequent refill opportunities are. Ensure you have enough carrying capacity to deal with the stretches between. A filter or other form of treatment might give you more flexibility in your water sources.
- If you are sweating a lot, think about replacing electrolytes. Tablets or powder can easily be added to your drink.
- Nighttime temperatures are often cooler. Consider finding somewhere shady for a nap during the day, and do most of your riding at the start and end of the day and even through the night.

COLD

How cold is cold? Many of the routes featured may see inclement weather. Regardless of the forecast, it is sensible to bring clothing that will keep you safe (if not totally comfortable) at the extremes you are likely to experience. Routes like the Iditarod take "cold" to the next level—but even if you aren't planning to ride in quite such freezing conditions, there are plenty of lessons to apply elsewhere.

- Hypothermia can strike almost any time; it doesn't need sub-zero temperatures. Learn to look for the signs in yourself and others.
- Layering is king. Multiple layers allow your body to work at an optimal temperature, whatever the conditions. Remember that sweat quickly soaks layers and will quickly chill you, so be careful not to overheat.
- Down offers a huge warmth-to-weight ratio and packs down small. The downside is it quickly loses its insulation properties when wet. Synthetic equivalents are rarely as warm for their size or weight but function much better when soggy.
- The colder conditions are, the stricter you need to be with self-care. Manage exposed skin, hydration, fueling, and overall comfort with an unyielding regimen.

ALTITUDE

Altitude is the great leveler. It has little regard for fitness and there are few shortcuts to dealing with its effects. Even the strongest of riders can find themselves brought to their knees, gasping for air on the simplest of climbs.

- If possible, spend some time acclimatizing. Our bodies are clever things, and will produce more red blood cells to deal with the reduction in oxygen.
- Give yourself time. Make sure your schedule allows for the inevitable slower pace that altitude brings.
- Sleep low. It might be tempting to enjoy summit views, but if you can, descend as far as possible to sleep. Our bodies struggle to rest and recover properly when starved of oxygen.
- Listen to your body. Headaches and nausea are to be expected—and only you know what level of discomfort you are willing to put up with—but learn to look for the signs of altitude sickness, and familiarize yourself with the risks.

TESTING LIMITS IN ALASKA'S WILD

ROUTE:
IDITAROD TRAIL

LOCATION:
UNITED STATES

IMAGINE RIDING YOUR BIKE in conditions so extreme that the grease in your hubs begins to freeze as you pedal through deep snow. You hold your breath as frozen river ice creaks under your weight, and when you do eventually exhale the moisture crystallizes on your face mask instantly. The short Alaskan day begins to draw to a close, and as the sun dips below the horizon, you focus on the thin rut left by a snowmobile that represents your trail. You block out the hundreds of miles left to go and focus on the warmth that the next checkpoint promises, just as you hear the howling of wolves in the distance …

The Iditarod Trail—which crosses wide tracts of empty Alaskan wilderness—was originally used for hundreds of years by the Native Alaskan Iñupiat and Athabaskan people, but traffic on the trail reached its peak between the late 1880s and mid-1920s as Russian fur traders, then coal and gold miners made the journey in search of riches. During the summer, the northern port of Nome, sitting on the Bering Sea, was accessible by steamship, but come winter—as the sea froze—dog sleds were needed to transport people and supplies.

Those sleds inspired "the father of Iditarod" Joe Redington Sr. to stage the Iditarod Trail Sled Dog Race along the 1,610 kilometers (1,000 miles) between Anchorage and Nome in 1973. He then decided to open up the event to human-powered entrants in 1987, including 26 riders who completed a 322-kilometer (200-mile) out-and-back race on a section of the trail. In doing so, the Iditarod became the first bikepacking race in the world, pitching cyclists against temperatures that can reach -40 °C (-40 °F).

Given the extreme conditions, it is perhaps not surprising that it took until 2000 for the first "Iditasport Impossible" (now renamed Iditarod Trail Invitational 1000) to pitch riders against the full length of the route from Anchorage to Nome. Many of the original settlements along the route died out when air travel became an option, but a handful remain. These now act as checkpoints for the race, with the wild Alaskan mountains and plains in between. It is testament to the size of the challenge that it is incredibly rare for people to tackle the ride outside of the race, and those that do have extensive knowledge of the route. On a typical year, only a handful of racers finish.

Riders depart Anchorage in March—any earlier and the river crossings may not yet have frozen, making the journey impossible. Temperature dictates so much when it comes to the Iditarod. In "warm" conditions (around 0°C/32°F) the snow can become mushy and heavy to pedal or push through. There's an increased risk of open water too. It's also much harder for riders to regulate their body temperature; sweat →

"ASK ANYONE WHO HAS COMPLETED THE EVENT AND THEY'LL TELL YOU IT IS A JOURNEY OF SURVIVAL FIRST AND FOREMOST."

← HUGE TIRES AT LOW PRESSURE ARE LIKE SNOW SHOES FOR BIKES.
→ IN DEEP WINTER THE SUN ONLY RISES FOR A FEW HOURS A DAY.
↓ THE IDITAROD TRAIL'S HERITAGE IS ACTUALLY IN DOG-SLEDDING, GIVEN IT WAS THE BEST WAY OF TRAVELLING ACROSS TUNDRA, THROUGH WINTER CONDITIONS.

ANCHORAGE TO NOME IS A HISTORIC ROUTE— SECTIONS OF WHICH WERE ORIGINALLY USED BY NATIVE ALASKAN PEOPLES. THE ROUTE WAS FURTHER ESTABLISHED AS A RESULT OF COAL MINING AND THE GOLD RUSH AROUND THE TURN OF THE CENTURY.

"RIDERS ENCOUNTER ASTONISHINGLY BEAUTIFUL WILDERNESS LANDSCAPES AND EMPTINESS ON A SCALE FOUND IN VERY FEW PLACES IN THE WORLD."

is a killer, especially if colder weather subsequently blows in. At the other end of the scale, the brutal lows usually mean faster riding conditions, but that the air is too cold to breathe directly while exercising, necessitating a mask. Exposed flesh is at high risk of frostbite (especially if it comes into contact with metal), and gas stoves cease to function as it is too cold to create a vapor to ignite.

Ask anyone who has completed the event, and they'll tell you it is a journey of survival first and foremost. Fresh snowfall can leave the trail unrideable, meaning hours of pushing a heavily laden bike through waist-high drifts. Even during clement conditions, simple tasks like eating and drinking take more effort than normal (adding layers when stopped, melting water, etc.) and during bad weather a mundane mechanical issue could be life-threatening. Delve into firsthand accounts and you'll find plenty of wild stories of bikes being thrown by rogue gusts of wind or metal parts shearing in extreme cold.

It's enough to make you question why anyone would take on such an event. Well, beyond the "because it's there" personal challenge, riders encounter astonishingly beautiful wilderness landscapes and emptiness on a scale found in very few places in the world. And while no landscape truly stays the same, the journey along the Iditarod Trail is more ephemeral than most. Tire tracks can fill in as soon as they are left and a few short months later, the blanket of white recedes until next year. The Iditarod gives participants the opportunity to sample life on the edge of what is humanly possible and complete a journey that only a select few will ever experience. ○

POGIES, A COLD-WEATHER KIT, AND EXPERIENCE ARE ESSENTIAL FOR RIDING DURING THE HARSH ALASKAN WINTER.

SURVIVAL MODE. WIND CHILL MEANS TEMPERATURES CAN DROP TO WELL BELOW -50°C (-58°F)—SWEAT AND HUB GREASE FREEZE INSTANTLY, AND AIR SAPS FROM TIRES.

ROUTE NOTES

Start: Anchorage, Alaska, USA / **Finish:** Nome, Alaska, USA / **Distance:** 1,610 km (1,000 mi)—a 563 km (350 mi) version is also available / **Duration:** 10–25 days, depending on conditions / **Category:** Multiday nonstop race / **Terrain:** Snow / **Level:** Extremely difficult

HIGHLIGHTS:

As well as the beautiful remoteness of the route, there is true camaraderie among the riders. Racing takes a back seat to the hardships of day-to-day survival and forward progress. And among the toil treasured, moments are discovered—whether that is the glory of a perfect sunrise or something more deeply personal.

WILDLIFE AND LANDSCAPE:

Wolves, moose, and caribou endure the full harshness of the Alaskan winter, but sightings are infrequent.

RESUPPLY NOTES:

While most bikepacking races are unsupported (no bag drops or organized support), the route has checkpoints spaced out at around 70 km (44 mi) intervals. These offer respite from the weather, a chance for some warm food and a few hours' sleep before riders step back out into the freezer.

ACCOMMODATIONS:

Some checkpoints offer basic lodging. Racers are required to carry full camping essentials.

GETTING THERE (AND BACK):

Fly to Anchorage. Return flights can be arranged upon arrival in Nome.

RIDE SEASON AND CLIMATE:

March. Extremely cold climate.

EQUIPMENT:

Large mandatory kit list; almost every single piece of equipment taken will be specialist gear, specifically chosen for the unique challenges of the event. Think expedition-weight insulated clothing and sleeping bag, riding boots that are several sizes too big to fit extra insulation under, and adjustments to almost every single component of the bike.

WHAT TO RIDE:

The Iditarod is what fat bikes were invented for—5-in. tires at extremely low pressures float on the snow and provide traction where nothing else will.

OTHER IMPORTANT INFORMATION:

You've probably already guessed that the ITI is not to be taken lightly. As well as the immensely difficult conditions, there is no defined trail; just GPS coordinates of checkpoints. Riders must demonstrate prior experience of dealing with similar conditions, and those wanting to ride the full 1,000 mi must have already completed the shorter 350-mi route.

ROUTEMAKER:

First devised by Joe Redington Sr.

CONTRIBUTOR INFO:

RJ Sauer is a writer, photographer, and filmmaker based in Vancouver, Canada. He loves to explore new places on bike.

USA
ALASKA
NOME
ANCHORAGE
BERING SEA
GULF OF
ALASKA
N

EXPERIENCE THE ANDES

ROUTE:
PERU DIVIDE

LOCATION:
PERU

IF THE HIMALAYAS ARE THE GREATEST mountain range in the Northern Hemisphere, the Andes are the greatest range in the Southern. The longest continental mountain range in the world, they stretch from Venezuela in the north to Argentina in the south, forming a continuous highland across South America. Their rocky pinnacles, crystal-clear lakes, and high-altitude plateaus are the stuff of adventure guidebooks the world over. Sitting just in the northern half of the range, the Peru Divide distills the pleasures of a continent-length mountain range into a visually stunning month on two wheels.

The route was first recorded by British couple Neil and Harriet Pike in 2013. The pair are experts on South American geography and have charted numerous routes around the Andes, including the Santo Toribio Circuit, the Huayhuash and Puya Raimondii Loop, and the Cordillera Blanca Circuit—many of which can be added to the Peru Divide if time permits. Alternatively, the modularity of the route means it can be tailored if necessary—the route is bisected by some "major" roads to large Peruvian cities. For many, the highlight is Huaraz to Huancavelica, which can be ridden in under three weeks, assuming proper acclimatization. Over the past decade, the route has developed into a badge of honor for touring cyclists, with travelers heading there from all over the world.

For most, the attraction is the astonishing landscapes. Mountains in the Southern Hemisphere are very different from those typically seen in the north. For Ben Johnson, who rode the route in 2019, this was what drew him to Peru: "I was struck with how vertical it looked and how diverse the landscapes were," he says. "I thought, maybe I should bikepack Peru? I had never bikepacked before, but I couldn't shake the idea."

The Divide begins in Huaraz, which is a local climbing hub. Access to and from Huaraz is simple, and it's a well-stocked hive of activity. Riders with little time should acclimatize here for at least three days before setting out on the route, while those with more time can explore the surrounding area extensively.

The route is primarily made up of long-abandoned access roads for mines, so it's chiefly twin-track gravel roads that are suitable for 4 × 4s. While some sections of chunky rock might require the odd push (especially on steeper ramps), the vast majority of the route consists of smooth dirt roads. There are some especially tough sections, however, with short sections simply hacked into the side →

THE STEEP, FLUTED SIDES TO THE MOUNTAINS ARE HALLMARKS OF SOUTH AMERICAN RANGES.

LOCAL GUESTHOUSES OFFER WELCOME RESPITE IF THE WEATHER TURNS.

“THE PERU DIVIDE DISTILS THE PLEASURES OF A CONTINENT-LENGTH MOUNTAIN RANGE INTO A VISUALLY STUNNING MONTH ON TWO WHEELS.”

of the mountain for mining access—those will require some time spent walking your bike. Amazingly, the routes give access to some of the most breathtakingly beautiful vistas on earth, but they do raise other questions—especially regarding the damage that mining has caused to the local area.

Because of the extreme nature of the route, bumping into riding companions, or even locals for that matter, is unlikely. Riders who have tackled the route speak of the solitude; locals refer to the ambiance in the high Andes as "el silencio," an eerie silence in which the only noise on the wind is the sound you make yourself.

Large swathes of the route are empty. Proper settlements where you can buy food are sporadic and often made up of just a few houses. For that reason, food and water autonomy is essential, as is a collection of spare bicycle parts and the knowledge of how to use them. Except for Huancavelica, which sits on the route, opportunities to get out cash are also few and far between. Other than the odd bit of food or occasional accommodations, there's almost nothing to spend money on so high in the mountains, but it's still best to be prepared. Small denomination notes of the sol are best (10s or 20s) but many places will also happily accept American dollars. A night in a basic *hospedajes* should cost around $5. →

PUYA RAIMONDII, QUEEN OF THE ANDES, IS NATIVE TO THE HIGHEST PLACES IN PERU.

AT 4,947 METERS (16,230 FEET), THE 600-METER (1,970-FOOT) CLIMB UP TO ABRA RITIPATA IS THE HIGHEST POINT OF THE ROUTE.

"I THOUGHT, MAYBE I SHOULD BIKEPACK PERU? I HAD NEVER BIKEPACKED BEFORE BUT I COULDN'T SHAKE THE IDEA."

As you might also expect for a route so remote, it's not marked on the ground. A GPS device with the route preloaded is essential, especially as a mobile phone signal is difficult at the best of times. That said, in many sections there will be just the one route across the mountain pass, so it's hard to go too wrong.

Four weeks to travel 1,600 kilometers (994 miles) might seem extravagant—around 50 kilometers (30 miles) per day—but the elevation is what slows people down. Many days are in excess of 2,000 meters (6,500 feet) of climbing, and rarely less than 1,000 meters (3,300 feet), with the whole route covering more than 40,000 meters (131,200 feet) of up and down—about what riders would cover in a typical running of the Tour de France. Many of the individual passes exceed 4,800 meters (15,750 feet), which is more than high enough to struggle with a lack of oxygen. "The biggest challenge for me was the altitude," says Ben. "The highest point I reached was 4,900 meters [16,076 feet]. Some days it took me hours to get my camp packed up. I would highly recommend getting used to riding steep gravel grades of 7 percent or more for long periods of time—or be happy to push your bike long distances, which I also did!" ○

MOST OF THE LOCAL ECONOMY IS FARMING, INCLUDING THE NATIVE ALPACA FOR ITS WOOL.

THE WILD HAIRPINS ARE THE RESULT OF MINING ROADS BUILD TO ACCESS INCREDIBLY REMOTE POCKETS.

ROUTE NOTES

Start: Huaraz, Peru / **Finish:** Abancay, Peru / **Distance:** 1,600 km (994 mi) / **Duration:** 4 weeks / **Category:** Multi-week expedition / **Terrain:** Wide gravel tracks, 90 % unpaved, nearly 100 % rideable / **Level:** Some off-road skills required but nothing technical

HIGHLIGHTS:

Compared to major Western conurbations, the route can be described as virtually traffic free. That means you can enjoy every moment of the long climbs and the roller-coaster descents. Riders who do the full route pick out the Cañete Valley, with its series of mini waterfalls, as one of the biggest highlights. Travelers with more time, especially for off-the-bike activities, should consider exploring the Cordillera Blanca.

LOCAL SPECIALTIES:

Mountain food is often basic, and in Peru, it's no different. Expect a staple of rice and fried eggs with the option to add chicken if you're lucky. Occasionally fresh fish, such as local trout, will appear on the menus in larger settlements.

WILDLIFE AND LANDSCAPE:

Peru is known for its high-altitude moonscapes and seemingly barren mountainsides. Spend more than a day or two riding, and it soon becomes clear there's no such thing as flat. Some climbs are days in the making, with subsequent descents lasting hours. Front to back, the route takes in nearly 40,000 m (131,200 ft) of climbing with many passes over 5,000 m (16,400 ft).

RESUPPLY NOTES:

Simple resupply places are regular along the route, but a minimum of two days' worth of supplies is recommended. Huancavelica, which sits just beyond halfway, is the perfect place to recharge for a day and stock up on supplies.

ACCOMMODATIONS:

Guesthouses can be found along the route with simple dorm rooms if the weather is poor. Most people choose to wild camp, which is easy as there are plentiful options.

GETTING THERE (AND BACK):

Fly to Lima, then from there, Cruz del Sur runs an overnight bus to Huaraz, which can be booked online. There is a fee for a bike, and it must either be wrapped up or boxed. They also offer a return to Lima from the finish in Abancay.

RIDE SEASON:

The Divide is best attempted from May to September, when average rainfall is lower and the climate is most stable. November to March is Peru's rainy season, which is famous for huge downpours and localized flooding, so best avoided.

EQUIPMENT:

Temperatures overnight can plunge into the minus single digits, so a sleeping bag that will go down to -6 °C (21 °F) is advised, as is a warm jacket/headgear for the mornings and evenings. Otherwise, it's best to pack as light as possible, given the amount of climbing.

WHAT TO RIDE:

The primary challenges are the elevation and long climbs, rather than the rough terrain. A gravel bike or touring bike with tires over 40 mm (1.5 in) will suffice. Regardless of the bike chosen, it must be geared for long periods of constant, relatively steep (over 5 percent) gradients. For some, this will mean a mountain bike.

IMPORTANT INFO:

Much of the route runs through high altitudes, and altitude sickness is to be respected. As long as plenty of time is given to acclimatize, there should be no issues. Cell service is patchy along the route, even with a local SIM card.

ROUTEMAKER:

The Peru Divide was devised by British couple Neil and Harriet Pike in 2013. The Pikes are experts in South American expeditions and have created many routes throughout the Andes.

CONTRIBUTOR INFO:

Ben Johnson is a multidisciplinary artist and designer. He rode the route solo in 2019.

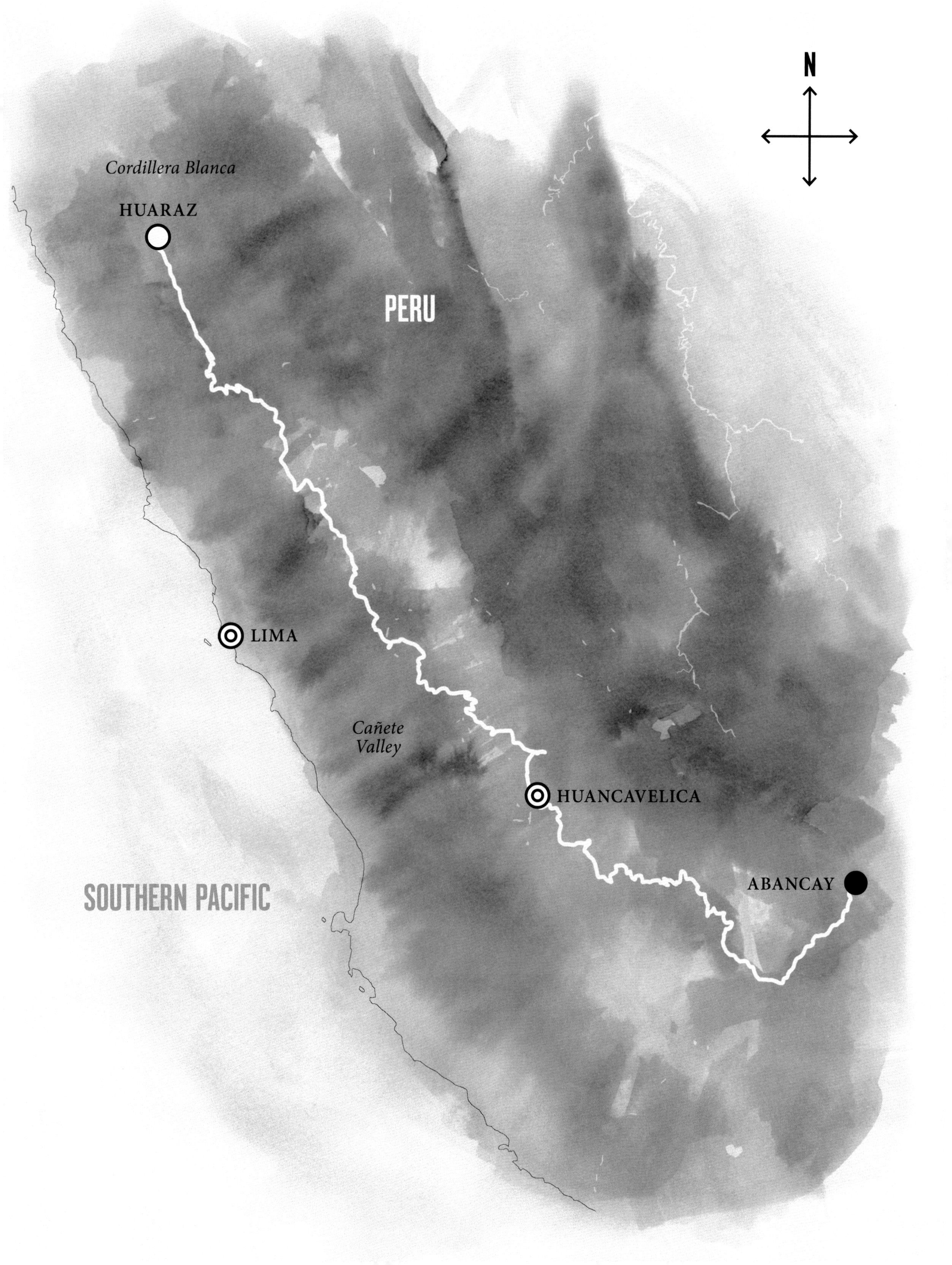
N
Cordillera Blanca
HUARAZ
PERU
LIMA
Cañete Valley
HUANCAVELICA
ABANCAY
SOUTHERN PACIFIC

TRAVERSING NATIONAL HISTORY

ROUTE:
LA RUTA MALA

LOCATION:
CUBA

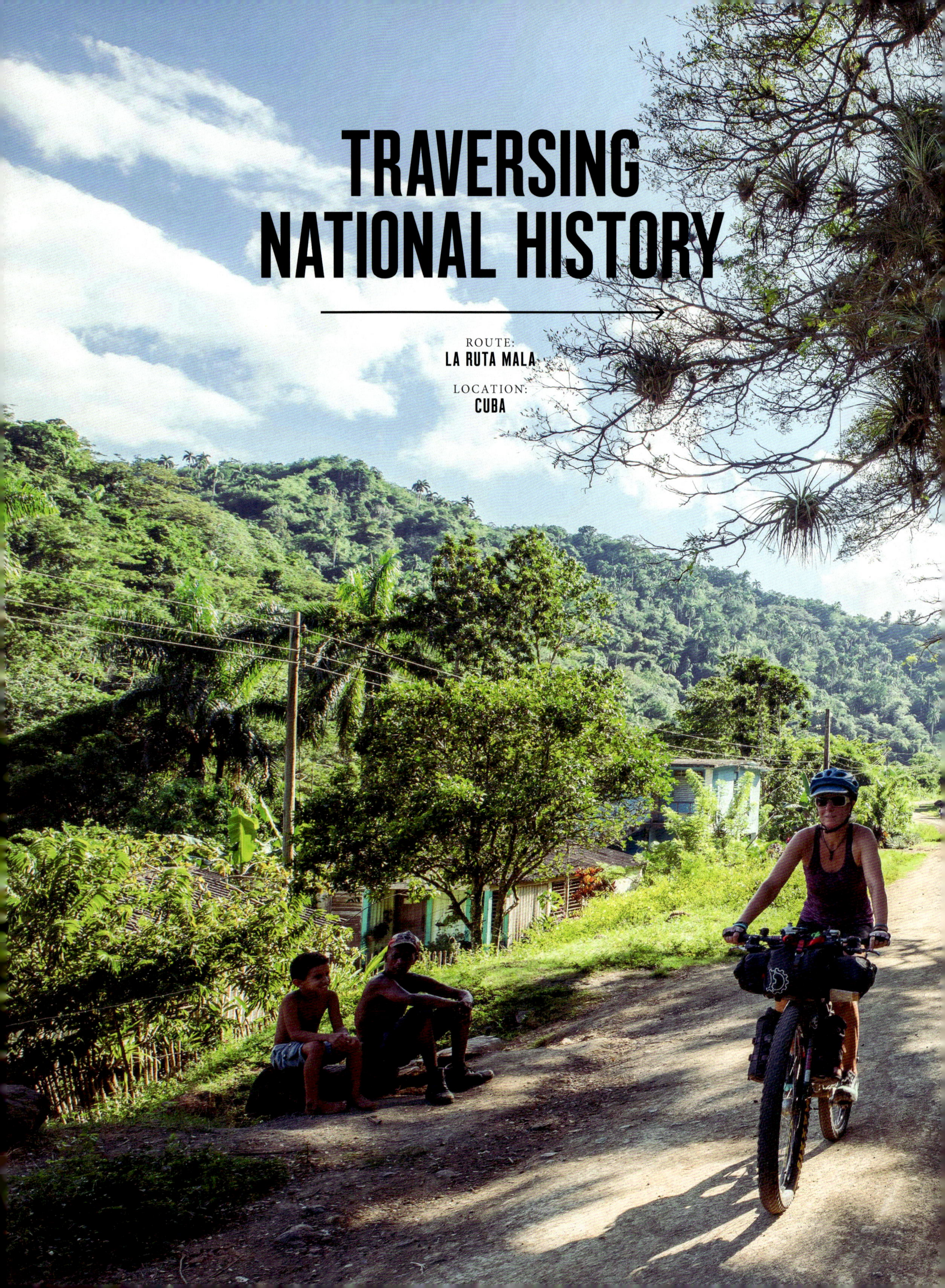

THERE ARE ROUTES that should be ridden for the technical challenge they provide, or the stunning scenery they cut through. La Ruta Mala should be ridden for the unique cultural insight it provides into Cuban life and the people encountered along the way.

As long-distance bikepacking routes go, La Ruta Mala (or Trans-Cuba as it's sometimes known) is in its relative infancy. Concocted by Logan Watts and Joe Cruz, it was designed to provide a novel way of crossing the country from east to west, while avoiding the well-worn tourist areas. The route was refined on the ground by the pair, who surprised even themselves when they discovered many of the tracks had likely never been tackled on two wheels before. Writing about the route, Watts says: "Joe Cruz and I designed it by poring over satellite imagery, a couple of paper maps, blogs, and trip reports by other bike tourists." While battling their way down many a rutted road, locals would stop and tell them they were going "the bad way," or more accurately, they were going "la ruta mala," Watts says. "We smiled and told them that we prefer the bad way."

Sitting just off the coast of Florida, and next to the Bahamas, the Cayman Islands, and Jamaica, Cuba combines a tropical climate with Caribbean culture and a unique style born from its fascinating and tumultuous recent history. As one of the few communist countries remaining, the cars and buildings hark back to a bygone area while some everyday items such as televisions and phones date back to the 1960s when the nation played a defining role during the Cold War. That turbulent past makes it one of the best countries to experience by bike. Riders can really immerse themselves in Cuba's complex history and cultural influences, meet local people, and experience the real Cuba far from the tourist-thronged main strips.

The route begins in Santiago de Cuba, a small city on the southeast coast, slowly winding its way through towns, villages, and countryside to the rural town of Viñales, taking in key moments from Cuba's history along the way. The route itself is mostly dirt tracks that would accommodate a 4 × 4, but there's also some tarmac, some gravel roads, and even a small amount of singletrack. While tourism is a growing industry in Cuba, cycle tourism is still rare, and those that do tend to stick to the roads, so it's unusual to meet another cyclist along the route.

Navigation on the ground can at times be rather difficult. In some places, there is only one routable option, but from season to season, these routes can be impassable mud or completely overgrown. It's best to have good-quality digital maps, and the freely available Open Street Map has good local information. If the tracks are truly terrible, most locals will give advance warning—even with the →

“RIDERS CAN REALLY IMMERSE THEMSELVES IN CUBA’S COMPLEX HISTORY AND CULTURAL INFLUENCES, MEET LOCAL PEOPLE AND EXPERIENCE THE REAL CUBA.”

← KARST MOUNTAINS FORM AS WATER ERODES THE SOFT LIMESTONE.
→ STICKY AND SWEET TWISTED BUNS ARE A LOCAL FAVORITE.
↓ TRAVELLERS ARE GREETED BY THE WARM AZURES OF THE CARIBBEAN SEA.

EVEN THE MODERN PARTS OF CUBA'S TOWNS HAVE A TRADITIONAL MID-CENTURY FEEL.

language barrier. Earlier in the season, waist-deep mud has been encountered, turning a fast-running trail into a multi-hour trudge. "Sometimes it's hard to get an objective answer when you ask how bad it is, especially with the language barrier," says photographer Mark Watson. "But when a lady holds her hand above her knees to show you the level, you know it's bad."

When the route isn't winding up forested mountains or along dusty trails, the towns are the places to soak in the culture. Along the route are Sancti Spíritus, Manzanillo, and Cienfuegos, particular highlights for their old-fashioned boulevards and local way of life where music, art, and dancing spill into the street. Camagüey is famous for its deliberately confusing road layout, designed to deter pirates after years of sustained raids.

Food and drink along the route can be difficult to come by at times, especially typical grocery staples. Fruit is in plentiful supply in the towns and villages along the route, but packaged food, such as cereal bars, can be hard to find. In most places, it's a case of eating as the locals do, and the guesthouses (known as *casas particulares*) offer a welcome respite with their famously plentiful breakfasts. Some even do evening meals, and most will serve killer mojitos.

As well as the cultural experiences along the route, the scenery is breathtaking, with fresh encounters promised daily. The route takes in not only the stunning Caribbean coast but three prominent mountain ranges, where the main challenge is not just the long, steady climbs but also the intense tropical heat. ○

AWAY FROM THE COAST, THE BEACHES GIVE WAY TO VAST AND MOUNTAINOUS TROPICAL FORESTS.

ROUTE NOTES

Start: Santiago de Cuba, Cuba / **Finish:** Viñales, Cuba / **Distance:** 1,384 km (860 mi) / **Duration:** 2–3 weeks / **Category:** Multi-week traverse / **Terrain:** Rugged dirt tracks, 80 % off-road, 10,000 m (32,808 ft) of ascent / **Level:** Some off-road skills required

HIGHLIGHTS:

There are the giant stretches of coastal waters that were host to 19th-century naval battles; Che Guevara's hideouts where he plotted Cuba's revolution; the beach where the U.S.-backed forces attempted their Bay of Pigs invasion; and more recently the remains of the collapse of the sugar industry from the Special Period of economic hardship.

LOCAL SPECIALTIES:

Flans are a commonly consumed food, often served both day and night in all manner of vessels—including in the bottom of a cut-off beer can. Most places make a delicious mojito, if that's your sort of thing.

WILDLIFE AND LANDSCAPE:

The mountain roads are lined with greenery—much more so than the coastal regions, which are lined with succulents and scrub. Then there are the famous palm trees that dot the landscape across the island, giant fronds swishing in the breeze. And the entire ride is worth it just for the giant limestone karst mountains at the finish in Viñales, which burst from the valley floor like nowhere else on earth.

RESUPPLY NOTES:

Groceries can be hard to find, so bring your own cereal/energy bars. Outside of large towns, food is quite basic.

ACCOMMODATIONS:

Casas particulares are numerous, offering plenty of overnight options with breakfast for minimal cost and are the only real options for tourists other than hotels.

GETTING THERE (AND BACK):

Fly into Havana, then take an overnight bus to Santiago de Cuba; it's around a 12-hour drive and 900 km (560 mi) transfer. From the finish, it's roughly 180 km (112 mi) from Viñales to Havana.

RIDE SEASON:

The best time to cycle in Cuba is between December and May, once the hurricane season has passed.

EQUIPMENT:

Parts for modern bikes are virtually nonexistent, so it's important to bring any spares with you. Mosquito repellent is also essential.

WHAT TO RIDE:

A mountain bike would be the most comfortable option but a gravel bike with 650b tires (2-in. width minimum) would also suffice.

ROUTEMAKER:

Devised and developed by Logan Watts, founder of bikepacking.com, and Joe Cruz in 2016.

CONTRIBUTOR INFO:

Mark Watson is a New Zealand-based photographer and writer who specializes in landscape, adventure, and travel photography. Together with Hana Black, he spent four years cycling around the Americas, two weeks of which was spent riding La Ruta Mala.

N
FLORIDA
BAHAMAS
HAVANA
VIÑALES
CUBA
SANCTI SPÍRITUS
CIENFUEGOS
CAMAGÜEY
MANZANILLO
SANTIAGO
DE CUBA
CAYMAN ISLANDS
JAMAICA
HAITI

TRAVELING IN GROUPS

Bikepacking can be a magical solo escape that offers solitude, time to think, and time to reflect. There is also a sense of satisfaction to be achieved by completing a route alone—fixing your own problems and looking within to find motivation during tough moments. Having said all that, an experience shared is an experience amplified. The right riding partners will take nothing away from a solo approach—you still have to pedal the whole route yourself—but there is something deeply special about relationships forged on the trail. Here are some tips to make your group riding experience a smooth one.

PICKING PARTNERS
A successful team bikepacking trip starts long before you set off. Think about what you and your potential partners are looking to get out of a ride. Are you aiming for FKT pace, or stopping for photos and swim spots every other mile? Are you looking forward to roughing it in a bivvy bag on the side of a mountain or more attracted by the spa hotel in the valley? There's obviously nothing wrong with either approach, but make sure the group is all on the same page before you start.

PACE
In an ideal world, your riding partner(s) will be at a similar fitness level. If there is a big disparity, the fitter person should be prepared to walk more often and move more slowly than they are used to. It's their role to change their pace, not the responsibility of the slower rider to try to keep up.

Having said that, there will be times where you naturally drift into your own paces. Embrace that, but regroup regularly, and make sure all parties are ready to move on, not just the fastest (who has also had the longest rest).

Remember that the larger the group, the greater the propensity to stop, and the longer those stops will take. Individual toilet breaks, mechanicals, and differing fitness levels all add up. Where possible, try to slot into a group rhythm and make the most of impromptu pauses to eat a snack or fix that niggling squeak. Whatever you do, try not to be that person who decides they need to do something urgent after everyone has just gotten ready to ride again.

WELLBEING
Check on each other regularly, and be empathetic. We all go through highs and lows during a long trip, and the beauty of riding in a group is that we can rely on others to pull us out of the lows. Be generous with your own mental energy when you have it to spare, and welcome help when you need it.

SHARING ITEMS
When traveling alone you obviously need to carry everything you think you'll need. Riding as a group affords a little flexibility to share some items. There is definitely no need for everyone to carry a stove for example. You might also want to think whether it is better to share a tent or use individual sleep systems. Some tools can be shared, but remember there is nothing more frustrating than getting a puncture and watching the rider with the pump disappearing down the trail (except perhaps being the rider that then has to hike back up with said pump).

CHANGE OF PLAN
Be prepared to rethink your plans if the group dynamic isn't working. This might mean cutting the route short, or it might mean splitting the group. It is better to finish a ride solo and still be friends, than to complete it together with a new-found foe. If you do decide to part ways, make sure both riders are completely self-sufficient, safe, and comfortable with this approach. If that's not the case, continue until it is suitable to do so, even if that is to the end of the route.

TRUE WILDERNESS IN A WEEK

ROUTE:
THE CROSS CAPE

LOCATION:
SOUTH AFRICA

WHEN RIDERS EMBARK on the Cross Cape route, what they're opening themselves up to is the sights, sounds, smells, and experiences of South Africa. Cutting across the middle of the country, the route offers cool ocean breezes, stunning views of wide-open spaces, sounds of exotic wildlife, and tastes of local and historical culture that can move you like nothing else.

That's why many riders don't describe it as a journey across South Africa but as a journey through the senses. A journey where your nostrils are filled by the smell of the fynbos (natural shrubland), where your mouth is stuffed with roosterbrood, and your eyes can barely take in the mountain vistas.

For Stan Engelbrecht, who has extensively explored the areas surrounding the cape, the variety of terrain is the real attraction: "The traverse from the sea to the top of the adjacent escarpment makes for some striking views," he says. As the name suggests, the route takes riders east to west through the heart of the Western Cape, from

GRAVEL TRACKS STRETCH OUT FOR MILES ACROSS THE CAPE.

the lush coastal Garden Route to the arid desert, across a mountain range, and through the world-famous grape growing regions. Most of the route follows smooth gravel tracks, although it does occasionally venture onto paved roads. Unlike some gravel routes, many of the tracks are the only way to travel from one village to the next, so while it's all low traffic, it's not entirely traffic free. You're just as likely, however, to share the road with animals as you are 4 × 4s. Even with the growth of adventure cycling, the likelihood of coming across fellow cyclists on the route is low, in part because there are just so many options for gravel travel.

One-third of the way into the route →

NO TRIP ACROSS SOUTH AFRICA WOULD BE COMPLETE WITHOUT A REFRESHING DIP.

"THE ABILITY TO WILD CAMP ALONG THESE ROUTES IS WHAT MAKES THEM A LOT MORE FUN AND CHALLENGING."

sits the famous, perhaps even infamous, Die Hel: a narrow and isolated valley 20 kilometers (12 miles) long and, in places, little more than a few hundred meters wide. The only thing the valley is known for other than its name, is its breathtaking beauty. Located in the Swartberg mountain range, it had been actively farmed from the 1800s, but it wasn't until early 1962 that a road was built into the valley. At points, the road drops for nearly 600 meters (2,000 feet) through a series of steep zigzags known informally as "the ladder." While Die Hel's official name is Gamkaskloof, a hybrid that combines Gamka (the Khoisan word for lion) and Kloof (the Afrikaans word for valley), it's from this hairpin road that the valley gained the colloquial moniker of Die Hel. It's believed the name comes from the Afrikaans word helling, or hel, which means steep—although another more exciting origin story is also told: supposedly, an animal inspector had to visit the valley in the 1940s before the proper road had been built and was forced to use a particularly arduous route. Having returned from his ordeal, he is said to have described it as a descent into hell. Needless to say, the name has spread into popular culture—a local mountain bike race that makes use of the valley is known as To Hell and Back.

As well as steep-sided valleys and mountain passes, the Cross Cape also has long stretches of arid quasi-desert with large →

IT'S CLEAR HOW THE ROAD DESCENT INTO DIE HEL GAINED ITS "LADDER" NICKNAME.

stretches of isolation. Compared to Europe or North America, where you're rarely more than a few miles from the next village (or person), there can be stretches in the Cross Cape where you might not see another person for an entire day.

For many riders this genuine experience of wilderness is a key attraction but also explains the local warmth when you do encounter other people. While bed-and-breakfasts and guesthouses can be found in most towns, many locals will quite happily invite you inside for a meal and perhaps even a bed. Even more intrepid explorers can camp along the route, and wild camping is a possibility in certain areas, as long as respect is paid to the local conditions. "For me, that is approaching true adventure," Stan says. "I would say the ability to wild camp along these routes is what makes them a lot more fun and challenging."

The route is publicized by a local government initiative, so route finding

THE AREA IS KNOWN FOR ITS VINEYARDS AS WELL AS ITS STUNNING SCENERY.

is easy. It's not signed on the ground, but good maps are available internationally and locally. There are also lots of background options on the ground, so it's possible to alter the route very simply to visit other attractions or to fit different timescales. A GPS device is still the best option for getting around simply, and the GPX file is available as a free download from the Cape Cycle Routes website.

Even leisurely riders can complete the full route in two weeks, but it's perfectly possible for fit riders to cover 100 kilometers (62 miles) per day and comfortably finish in seven days. ○

ROUTE NOTES

Start: Plettenberg Bay, South Africa / **Finish:** Stellenbosch, South Africa / **Distance:** 742 km (461 mi) / **Duration:** 1–2 weeks / **Category:** Multi-week, point-to-point / **Terrain:** Mainly gravel, 10,000 m (32,000 ft) of ascent / **Level:** Moderate

HIGHLIGHTS:

The route includes the spectacular Outeniqua, Swartberg, and Seweweekspoort passes, and the Cape Fold Mountains, with the ability to add sections along the coast. The route also includes typical Karoo (an Afrikaans word for a semi-desert region) towns that are very specific to South Africa, with the associated mix of culture and curiosities.

LOCAL SPECIALTIES:

Each area has a local delicacy, but most foods have evolved through need for preservation. Many will be familiar with biltong (dried meat), but there's also roosterbrood (bread prepared on an open fire), skuinskoek and koeksisters (sweet baked cakes in sugary syrup). The area is also famous for its craft beers and world-class wines.

WILDLIFE AND LANDSCAPE:

Mountain passes, huge valleys, dirt roads past miles of plateaus—the route has it all. South Africa is famous for its wildlife, with everything from impala to African elephants.

RESUPPLY NOTES:

Towns along the route will allow for easy resupply but they can be over 50 km (30 mi) apart, with little support in between. Riders need to carry everything with them including food, water, and shelter just in case. Parts and means to repair bikes are also essential.

ACCOMMODATIONS:

Every town along the route has charming little restaurants or bed-and-breakfasts that are run by friendly locals—each one completely unique. The popularity of the route is growing, but the areas are not heavily touristed, so establishments are always happy to receive visitors.

GETTING THERE (AND BACK):

Fly into Cape Town, then take a bus to Plettenberg Bay. Translux operates a daily bus, which takes approximately nine hours and costs around 300 Rand ($20). From Stellenbosch, there's a direct train, which takes 90 minutes and operates every two hours, with tickets from 8 Rand.

RIDE SEASON:

The South African climate is moderate and stable year-round. In the height of summer and depths of winter, it can be considerably hotter and cooler as you'd expect, but the route never becomes impassable. Even so, most riders will tackle the route between September and March.

EQUIPMENT:

The means to carry water and some water purification options, in case you need to source from a river. A minimum of 2–3 liters is recommended but some riders carry as much as 10 in hotter months.

WHAT TO RIDE:

The route is primarily gravel tracks, so either a gravel bike with chunky tires (over 50 mm) or a hardtail 29er mountain bike are ideal.

IMPORTANT INFO:

Unlike many routes across Europe, opportunities for resupply are few and far between, particularly for water. There's little infrastructure between towns, so special attention should be paid to water planning.

ROUTEMAKER:

Cape Cycle Routes curated the route in 2016 as an initiative by the Western Cape Government to turn the area into the premier cycling destination in Africa.

CONTRIBUTOR INFO:

Stan Engelbrecht is a photographer and publisher whose love for cycling as a means of reaching interesting places knows no bounds. He has traveled extensively around South Africa by bicycle.

N
SOUTH AFRICA
Gamkaskloof
(Die Hel)
Swartberg Pass
Seweweekspoort
STELLENBOSCH
PLETTENBERG
BAY
CAPE TOWN
Outeniqua Pass
SOUTH ATLANTIC

HIGH-ALTITUDE HOSPITALITY IN THE BARTANG VALLEY

ROUTE:
BARTANG VALLEY AND PAMIR HIGHWAY

LOCATION:
KYRGYZSTAN, TAJIKISTAN, AFGHANISTAN, AND UZBEKISTAN

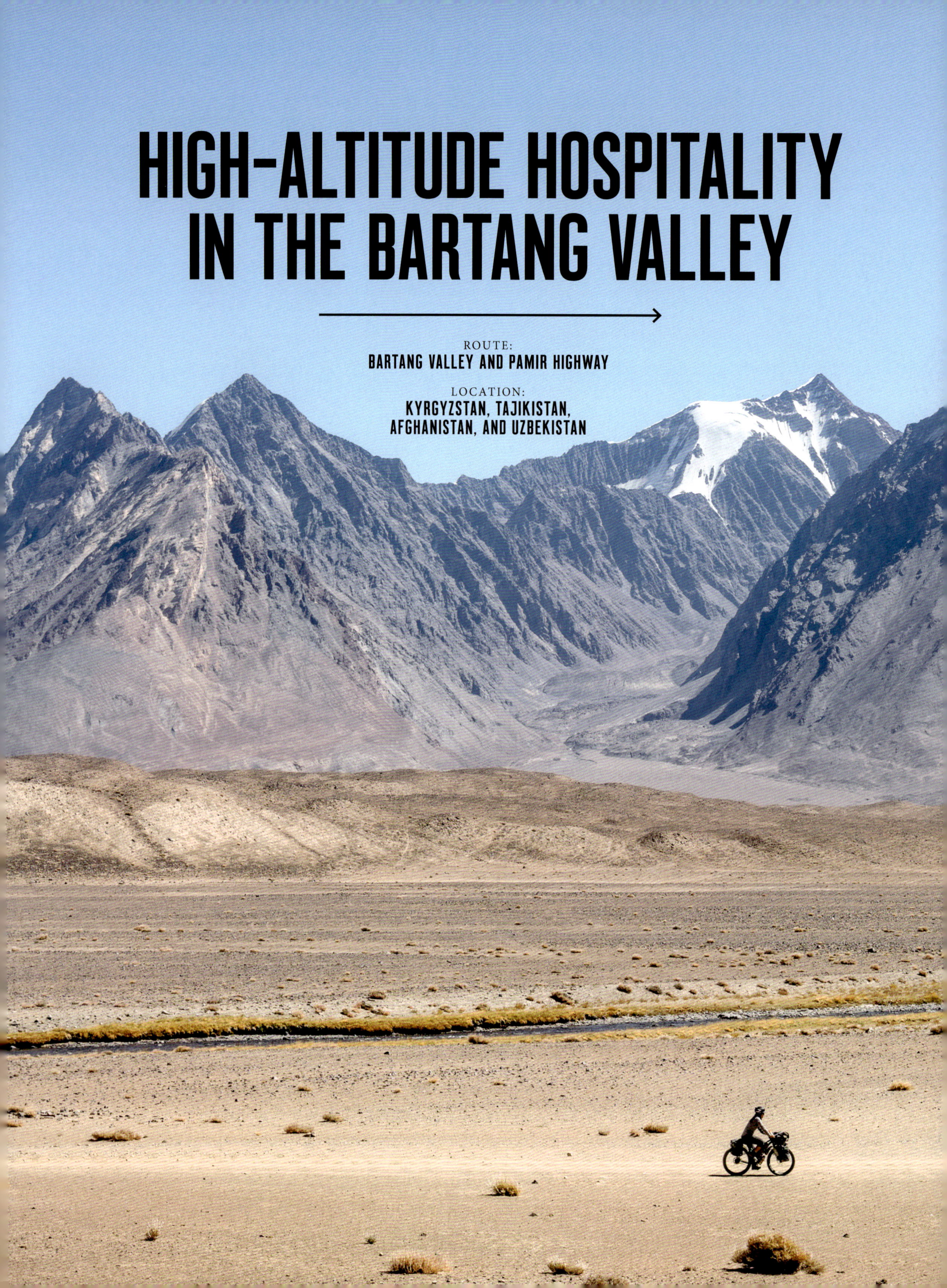

THE M41: A SHORT-LIVED URBAN MOTORWAY traversing Central London. The Pamir Highway: one of the most iconic bikepacking roads in the world.

While London's town planners were dreaming up an ultimately defunct (angry residents defeated the plans) cross-city motorway in the 1930s, the Soviets actually went ahead and built their M41, now better known as the Pamir Highway. It's a 1,252-kilometer (778-mile) route through Central Asia taking in Afghanistan, Uzbekistan, Tajikistan, and Kyrgyzstan, and is the second-highest road in the world, rising to 4,655 meters (15,272 feet) above sea level.

It's a massive challenge—make no mistake. Altitude affects people in different ways, and the weather is—unsurprisingly given the height—unpredictable. The route starts in Osh in southern Kyrgyzstan and heads through the Pamir Mountains, skirts along the border of Afghanistan, and finishes up in Dushanbe, the capital of Tajikistan.

It's a bucket-list route in its own right but is also the gateway to an even less-trodden and, to some bikepacking messiahs like Ryan Wilson, an even better adventure: the Bartang Valley. Ryan rode large chunks of the Pamir Highway and the full Bartang Valley as part of a larger tour through Kyrgyzstan, Tajikistan, Uzbekistan, and Kazakhstan. A former TV and film audio engineer, Wilson quit that day job to explore the world on two wheels full-time in 2016.

As a result, he is regularly asked what the number-one road or route he'd recommend riding on the planet is. His answer? Bartang.

While the Pamir Highway can be ridden on a regular touring-bike setup, the Bartang ideally needs a mountain bike and 2–3-in. tires. It also needs a fair bit of planning (the weather window is relatively tight: June to September), a comfort with life way, way off the beaten track, and a little bit of luck. If the weather is against you (think landslides, flooded rivers) the rocky, sandy tracks will not be your friend. The route is extremely remote, so don't expect to see many people. Your only real constant, reliable companion is altitude. More than half of the Bartang is spent above 4,000 meters (13,123 feet), with a high point of 4,280 meters (14,042 feet).

You get there by climbing your way up through a no-man's-land in between Kyrgyzstan and Tajikistan. The reward for that is the Murghab Plateau, a windy desert-meets-moonscape that eventually takes in the beautiful lakeside town of Karakul. There, you turn west off the M41 and you're on the Bartang route—a route that captured Ryan's heart in part for its combination of "just enough challenge with amazingly scenic and traffic-free roads."

What stood out above all, he says, was the overwhelming hospitality. →

"IT'S A BUCKET-LIST ROUTE IN ITS OWN RIGHT BUT IS ALSO THE GATEWAY TO AN EVEN LESS-TRODDEN AND AN EVEN BETTER ADVENTURE: THE BARTANG VALLEY."

← COLORFUL MOUNTAIN PEAKS SWELL AROUND THE VALLEY'S GRAVEL ROADS.
→ THE RUGGED BARTANG VALLEY IS SO DEVOID OF VEHICLES THAT IT FEELS LIKE IT WAS MADE JUST FOR BIKES.
↓ WILD CAMPING IS STUNNING, BUT LOCAL HOMESTAYS ARE A GREAT OPTION BECAUSE FOOD IS INCLUDED.

AT 4,655 METERS (15,270 FEET), THE PAMIR HIGHWAY IS THE SECOND HIGHEST MAIN ROAD IN THE WORLD. STOCK UP ON FOOD IN RUSHAN BEFORE RIDING THE BARTANG VALLEY ROUTE.

Wild camping is a viable option in Bartang, and there probably aren't many wilder places to pitch a tent in the world. However, Ryan and other Bartang veterans swear by the village homestays on the route. Between $10–15 buys you dinner, bed, and breakfast, a welcome reward given that the alternative is noodles, chocolate bars, and soda that will have been in your bike luggage for a good few days. (Stores are rare, and any choice other than packaged long-life options are even rarer.)

The food is secondary, however, to the window into another culture the homestays bring and the warm welcome you'll receive: "There are many rugged and beautiful roads to ride in the world," Ryan says, "but this level of hospitality is rare." Expect to be offered tea when riding by and people only too happy to break off from working in the fields to smile and greet you—and even, in Ryan's case, chase him down the road, proffering apples and walnuts.

The Pamir Highway and the Bartang take a bit of getting to, both logistically (you need a visa to enter Tajikistan, for example) and in terms of lung power. But the rewards are incredible. It is probably one of the last few truly remote places left in the world that feel, according to Ryan, "trapped in time." Ironically, for a valley that comes to a close in a place called Rushon, everything happens slowly—and with kindness and warmth. ○

PEOPLE ALONG THE BARTANG VALLEY LIVE SELF-SUFFICIENTLY—GROWING VEGETABLES AND REARING ANIMALS—A SHARP CONTRAST AND A REMINDER OF WHAT LIFE WAS ONCE LIKE.

"THERE ARE MANY RUGGED AND BEAUTIFUL ROADS TO RIDE IN THE WORLD, BUT THIS LEVEL OF HOSPITALITY IS RARE."

ROUTE NOTES

Start: Osh, Kyrgyzstan (Pamir)/Karakul, Tajikistan (Bartang) / **Finish:** Dushanbe, Tajikistan (Pamir)/Rushon, Tajikistan (Bartang) / **Distance:** Bartang Valley (415 km/258 mi), Pamir Highway (1,252 km/778 mi) / **Duration:** Bartang (5–7 days), Pamir (14–21 days) / **Category:** Multiday, point-to-point / **Terrain:** 77 % unpaved / **Level:** Difficult

LOCAL SPECIALTIES:

Homestay food. Each village grows what it needs to eat. Wilson regularly saw his hosts picking fresh vegetables from the garden before preparing them for meals. Apples, walnuts, and apricots abound.

WILDLIFE AND LANDSCAPE:

Keep your eye out for the Marco Polo sheep, named after the 13th-century explorer. They live in the mountainous regions of Central Asia and their horns are often found on the route.

RESUPPLY NOTES:

If eating well—and interestingly—is high on your list of priorities, then homestays will be your friend on the Bartang (see above). Stores are few and far between. You can buy supplies on the Pamir Highway in Sary-Tash (Kyrgyzstan) and then in Karakul and Khudara on the Bartang. Water, aside from on the Murghab Plateau, is not really an issue, but it's worth filtering to stay safe.

ACCOMMODATIONS:

Most of the villages on either route have homestays that include dinner and breakfast for 10–15. They also always include the warmest of welcomes—cycle tourists are some of the only visitors (especially in the Bartang Valley) and villagers welcome the chance for a chat in English (or Russian). Bartang is a haven for wild camping; pitch anywhere you want—literally, anywhere.

GETTING THERE (AND BACK):

Not easy. The nearest airport to the start of the Bartang at Karakul is in Osh (a three-hour taxi ride or two days' riding). To ride the Bartang, almost everyone takes in some of the Pamir Highway on the way. You'll leave the Pamir at around 4,000 m (13,123 ft) altitude, not long after Karakul, and rejoin five days or so later at Rushon. At the finish of the Bartang in Rushon, it's between 12–16 hours in a jeep taxi to Dushanbe (the capital of Tajikistan) or a week's riding along the Pamir Highway.

RIDE SEASON:

The best time to ride the Bartang is late summer to early fall (June to September). Avoid winter at all costs—temperatures in the Bartang Valley have been known to hit -60 °C (-76 °F).

EQUIPMENT:

Half the Bartang is spent at over 4,000 m (13,123 ft) altitude meaning even in summer, nights are cold. Your sleeping setup needs to reflect that if you're planning to camp. A sturdy pair of off-bike shoes is also useful for river crossings.

WHAT TO RIDE:

The Pamir has a generally decent surface (a mix of road and dirt) so usually attracts more traditional road or touring bike setups. Your bike will take a battering on the Bartang, so mountain bikes and 2–3-in. tires are a must.

CONTRIBUTOR INFO:

Ryan Wilson, a former audio engineer who, after a life-changing trip riding through the Andes in 2016, now spends all his time on two wheels, camera in hand.

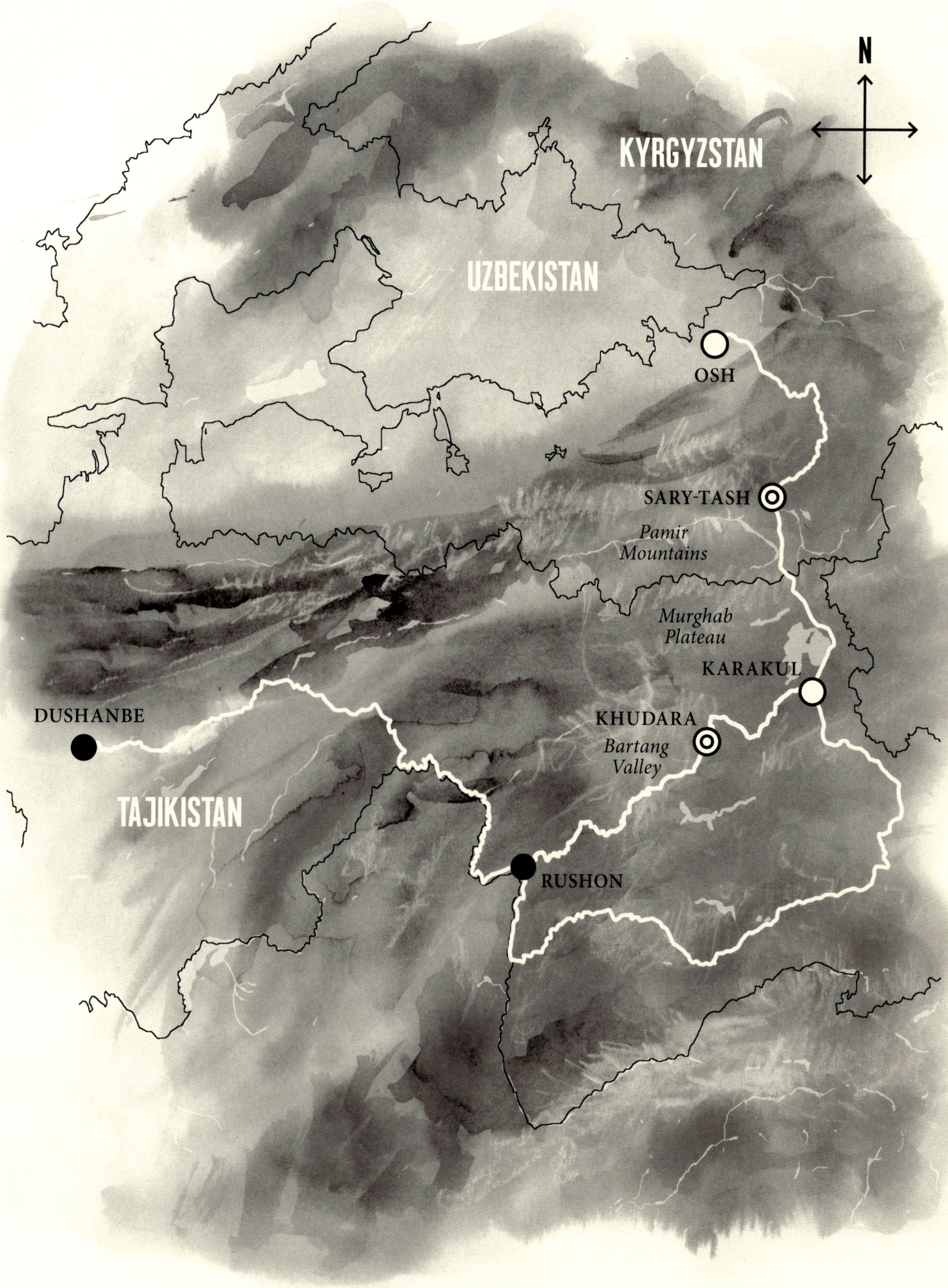
N
KYRGYZSTAN
UZBEKISTAN
OSH
SARY-TASH
Pamir
Mountains
Murghab
Plateau
KARAKUL
KHUDARA
Bartang
Valley
DUSHANBE
TAJIKISTAN
RUSHON

THE PLACES IN BETWEEN

ROUTE:
THE MIDDLE LANDS

LOCATION:
INDIA

↑ THE TAGLANGLA PASS IS INDEED VERY HIGH, BUT SINCE THE SIGN WAS MADE, IT'S BEEN DEMOTED TO 13TH HIGHEST.
→ THE NEWLY BUILT SECTIONS OF THE HIGHWAY ARE A TOURING CYCLIST'S DREAM.

SOME OF THE MOST FASCINATING PLACES, both geographically and politically, are those in-between areas. Sandwiched by impassable mountains, rivers, forests, or deserts lie whole villages, towns, and cities that develop their own ways of living. In the far north of India lies one of these places: the Spiti Valley.

Gaining its name from the Spiti River, which runs through the Himachal Pradesh region of India, the valley is sandwiched between China, Tibet, Pakistan, and Nepal. So it's perhaps no surprise that the Bhoti word *spiti* quite literally translates as "the middle land." Surrounded by mountains on all sides, and regularly cut off when the weather turns, the Spiti Valley is one of the least populated regions of India and also one of the most beautiful. A cycling mecca, the Middle Lands route connects the legendary NH3 Leh-Manali Highway with the NH505 to create a simply astonishing high-mountain traverse. "The barren yet colorful mountain world fascinated us from the beginning," says Sara Bukies, who, along with Andreas Krucker, tackled the route in 2019. "And of course it was a special challenge to repeatedly cross passes over 4,000 meters [13,123 feet]."

Beginning in the city of Leh, the NH3 snakes south to Manali before joining the NH505 and heading east to Nako, through the union territory of Ladakh and the state of Himachal Pradesh as well as the Ladakh and Zanskar mountain ranges, and, of course, the Kinnaur and Spiti valleys. Many riders choose to stay a few days in Leh to acclimatize—it's possible to take some gentle day trips to Buddhist monasteries while your body gets used to its new, low-oxygen diet.

Beginning with the popular Leh to Manali section, the route gradually sheds its greenery in favor of high alpine-style desert scenery. Given the altitude of the route and the passes involved, the biggest challenge is the lack of oxygen, but the road itself likes to throw up a few challenges too. While much of the route is either paved or smooth dirt, with gradients that stay in the single figures, the conditions can vary at times with rough stones and even the odd river crossing.

To reach the eastern end of the route, through upper Kinnaur and into the Spiti Valley, requires a government permit due to →

ANCIENT MONASTERIES
PUNCTUATE THE
RUGGED LANDSCAPE.

"SURROUNDED BY MOUNTAINS ON ALL SIDES, THE SPITI VALLEY IS ONE OF THE LEAST POPULATED REGIONS OF INDIA BUT ALSO ONE OF THE MOST BEAUTIFUL."

the sensitivity surrounding the Tibetan border. As tempting as it might be to just ride and hope for the best, the route has a significant army and police presence with checkpoints where it's impossible to avoid the document checks. The permit can be obtained in Delhi, Kullu, and Shimla, or along the route at Reckong Peo—the last town before the closed area. In a peculiar twist of bureaucracy, the permit is only available to groups of two or more, so solo travelers will need to find another in the same boat to team up. Oddly, you're not actually required to travel together; it's purely a formality for obtaining the permit. The cost is minimal—expect to pay 200 rupees (about $2).

If time permits, a visit off the route to the village of Kibber, which sits in its own nature reserve, is well worth it. Risking a trip on the Kibber cable car, however, is optional: "If you don't want to backtrack to the main route along the valley floor then →

LENTILS, RICE, AND CHAPATI ARE THE STAPLES OF ROADSIDE SUSTENANCE.

"THE BARREN YET COLORFUL MOUNTAIN WORLD FASCINATED US FROM THE BEGINNING."

you'll need 'balls of steel' as a friend exclaimed after seeing the photos," says photographer Mike Hayes. "The crossing to the village of Chichim involves a small steel basket suspended from a single cable that crosses a deep canyon about 100 m (300 ft) wide and a few hundred meters deep. Taking a bike requires finding someone in the village with some rope, so you can tie your bike to the outside of the basket and pull yourself across using a rope suspended from the cable. Not for the faint hearted!"

Sticking to the main route keeps navigation simple—while it's not signed as a cycle route, the route itself is signed, and there's often only one road anyway. Cell phone reception and internet access are virtually nonexistent while in the valleys, so routes are best downloaded in advance. As the routes are vehicular, most mapping software will plot the entire route without much trouble—meaning less time spent worrying about where the turns are, more spent gazing at the surroundings. ○

ROUTE NOTES

Start: Leh, India / **Finish:** Nako, India / **Distance:** 430 km (267 mi) / **Duration:** 8–10 days / **Category:** Multiday expedition / **Terrain:** Hard pack dirt tracks / **Level:** Some off-road skills required

HIGHLIGHTS:

The Kinnaur Valley is beautiful, with thousands of years of cultural history. The upper reaches are also relatively untouched as a government permit is required to visit. The Spiti Valley itself is breathtaking, with peaks either side that dwarf a touring cyclist.

LOCAL SPECIALTIES:

Like mountain food the world over, sustenance is basic but high in calories. Expect plenty of lentils, chickpeas, and paneer, mostly served with rice and flatbreads.

WILDLIFE AND LANDSCAPE:

The landscapes change considerably as the elevation increases, particularly in the Kinnaur Valley as the warmth and humidity of the lower slopes give way to the arid, cold desert further up. The area around Kibber is a nature reserve, home to blue sheep and snow leopards, although you're highly unlikely to see the latter.

RESUPPLY NOTES:

There are numerous smaller towns along the route where you can stock up on supplies and often stay the night. There are also plenty of dhabas, roadside stalls or cafes, where you can pick up basic dishes of rice, lentils, and sauce—and dal bhat if you're lucky. Off the route, a stove for hot drinks and warm food is best.

ACCOMMODATIONS:

Guesthouses line the route, so camping gear can be left at home. But if exploring some of the wild areas off the main highway, a tent is essential.

GETTING THERE (AND BACK):

You can fly to Delhi and take a bus to Leh, or fly to Chandigarh, where you can hire a private taxi for a transfer to Leh.

RIDE SEASON:

The route is only rideable from late May to late October, as the passes are closed in winter. The best time to travel is mid-August to mid-October to avoid high water and monsoon season.

EQUIPMENT:

A down jacket, warm gloves, and a hat are a must as overnight temperatures easily drop into the minus figures. If you're keen on coffee, you'll need to bring your own, as well as an espresso maker, as coffee is very hard to find in the north. Some medication, used to prevent and reduce the symptoms of altitude sickness, is also worth investigating.

WHAT TO RIDE:

As the roads in the Spiti Valley can be quite rocky, 2.1-in. tires are a minimum, which necessitates either a mountain bike or gravel bike. A hardtail 29 in. would provide the best balance of comfort and efficiency, especially on the paved sections of the Leh–Manali stretch.

IMPORTANT INFO:

As well as the usual concerns of altitude sickness and cold temperatures, rockfalls in the upper Kinnaur Valley are of particular concern. Avoid lengthy stops in this region.

HISTORY:

The area has been strategically important since the Kargil War between India and Pakistan in 1999 and is maintained by the Border Roads Organisation (BRO) of the Indian Army.

CONTRIBUTOR INFO:

Sara Bukies and Andreas Krucker run together Project Pedal Further. Mike Hayes is a Cornwall-based photographer.

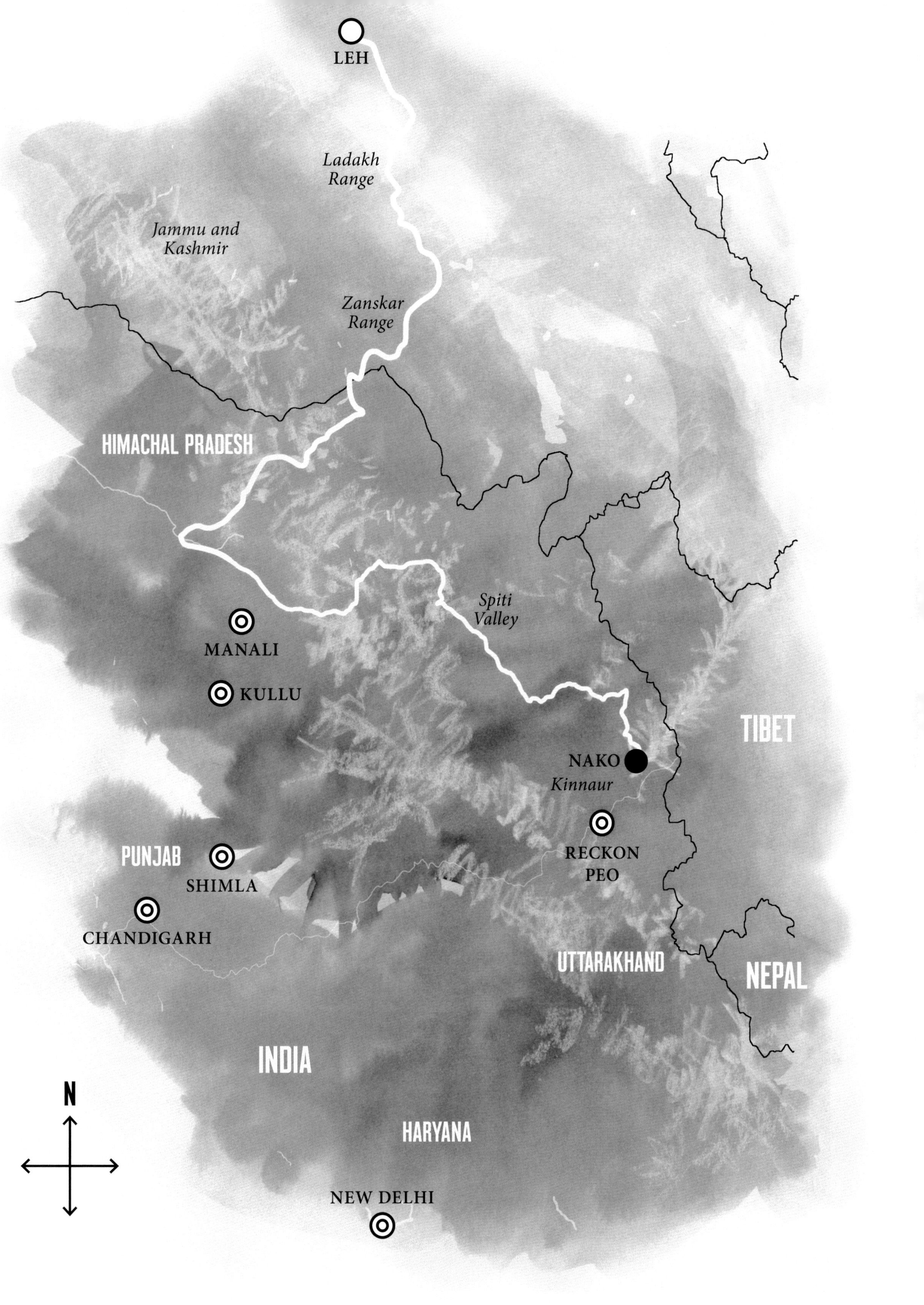
LEH
Ladakh Range
Jammu and Kashmir
Zanskar Range
HIMACHAL PRADESH
Spiti Valley
MANALI
KULLU
TIBET
NAKO
Kinnaur
RECKON PEO
PUNJAB
SHIMLA
CHANDIGARH
UTTARAKHAND
NEPAL
INDIA
N
HARYANA
NEW DELHI

TRAVELING IN REMOTE ENVIRONMENTS

Bikes are amazing tools for travel. They can carry us for miles each day and into some of the most remote places in the world. So it's important that we prepare sufficiently to minimize the chances of anything going awry and are able to fix the problem ourselves if at all possible—or at least get to safety. And when we do reach civilization, travel is most fulfilling when we connect with the people we meet.

NAVIGATION

Most of the routes featured are not sign-posted. Even if they are, at least one form of navigation is advised. A GPS device is the most straightforward to use when on the bike. It allows you to enjoy the actual riding while only keeping a cursory eye on your direction. Remember you will almost certainly need a method of charging your device over multiple days of travel. Also, consider what you will do if the device breaks. Carry a backup, whether that is maps on your phone (make sure they are downloaded to the phone and don't require reception to use) or old-fashioned paper.

SUPPLIES

The further into the wilds your route goes, the more self-sufficient you'll need to be.

- Bring enough food to more than last until you reach the next town.
- Dehydrated food packs the smallest and lightest for the number of calories, but you'll need a stove to heat water to make it edible.
- Bring a water filter or other purification system.
- Think about your shelter.

STAYING IN TOUCH

You may be out of contact with the outside world for days at a time. Enjoy and embrace the solitude, but also take some additional steps. Let loved ones know that you won't be reachable for a while. Arrange a day and time by which you'll make contact, and agree on a plan for what should be done if you don't. Pass on the contact details for local emergency services. Consider carrying a tracking device like a Garmin inReach or SPOT tracker. These are two-way GPS devices that will relay your location to the outside world. Many allow a preprogrammed message to be sent to a designated phone number and have an SOS button that will alert authorities in emergencies.

LANGUAGE AND CULTURE

When traveling abroad, learning even the most simple of local phrases can hugely enhance your experience. Be respectful of the communities you are passing through; this is their home. Understand and accept that their culture may be different from the one you are used to. Take the time to say hello to the people you meet, and never underestimate the power of a loaded bicycle to stimulate curiosity and conversation.

If you are riding through areas that have significantly less wealth than your own situation, be mindful of that. Haggling may be a normal part of their culture, but will a few cents really matter to you?

Welcome others' generosity and thank them for it but never expect or rely on it. Think about small gifts that you may be able to offer in return. Can you carry some stickers or something similar to give to children that you meet?

BIKEPACKING BENEATH HIMALAYAN HORIZONS

ROUTE:
ANNAPURNA CIRCUIT

LOCATION:
NEPAL

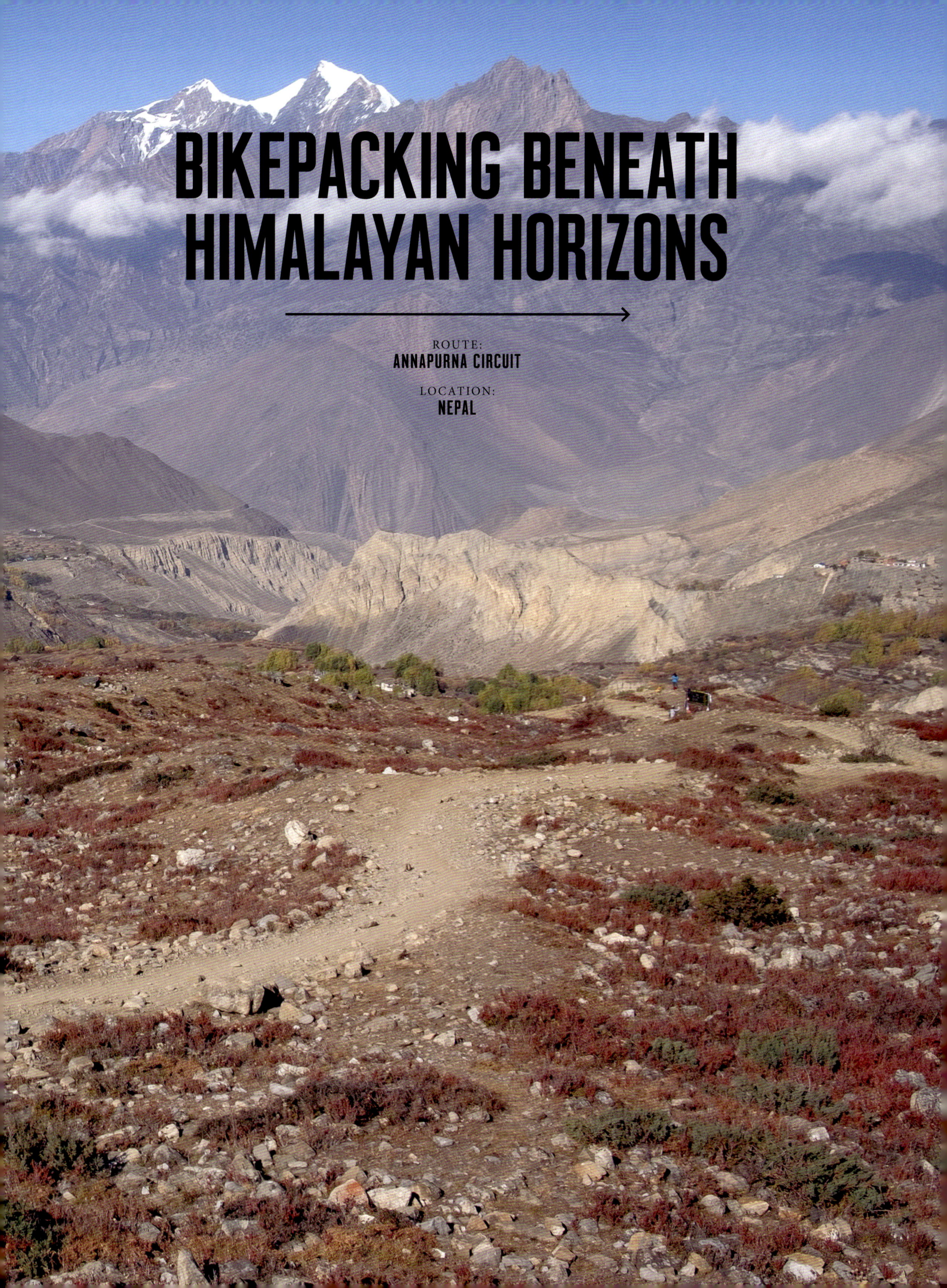

↑ FAT TIRES ARE KEY TO LIFE ON THE DIRT TRACKS OF NEPAL.
→ THE ANNAPURNA MASSIF DOMINATES THE GANDAKI PROVINCE.

STUDDING EVERY ROAD, highway, and thoroughfare around the Annapurna Circuit are sumptuous cafes serving local delicacies and steaming mugs of milk tea. Hives of activity, they punctuate the route and have turned the area—known for treacherous mountains, shimmering glaciers, and prayer flags dancing on the wind—from a wilderness to a welcome retreat. Riders come for the views and stay for the dal bhat.

Steeped in history, the Annapurna massif in northern Nepal is responsible for some of the greatest tales of the formidable high mountains. Sitting approximately 55 kilometers (34 miles) across, the massif is bordered by pockets of nature in every direction, including the Pokhara Valley to the south, the Kali Gandaki Gorge to the west, and the Marshyangdi River, which runs north to east. With it, the river brings water and life to the surrounding areas and explains how the massif took its name from the Hindu goddess Annapurna: the "giver of food and nourishment."

At the heart of the massif sits the highest peak of Annapurna I Main. With an 8,091-meter (26,545-foot) peak, it is the 10th-highest mountain on earth and was the first of the "eight-thousanders" to be conquered. Scan the skyline and you're unlikely to be able to pick out the main peak itself. So terrible were the maps until 70 years ago that it took the first successful expedition nearly two weeks just to find the mountain. Now things are much simpler, and since the late 1970s, the Annapurna Circuit has become a well-known route with few surprises, making it ideal for those who want to experience the joy of the high mountains for the first time.

No world tour of the high mountains can exclude the Himalayas. Along the way, riders are treated to mountain views, diverse scenery, welcoming culture, and some of the best opportunities to get up close and personal with the 8,000-meter (26,247-foot) giants. Unlike some of the mountainous circuits elsewhere, the Annapurna Circuit is unique in that there's no true solitude and no silent nights under the stars because of the sheer level of outside tourism. But that does come with the advantages of offering the vastness of the earth's natural wonders without having to abandon civilization for weeks on end.

For the most part, the locals speak good English—especially those under 30 years of age—and those who don't are well versed in the international system of point left, point right, wiggly hand for bumpy, and forearm at 45 degrees for steep. →

Given the circuitous nature of the route, there's only really one navigational decision that needs to be made in advance: clockwise or counterclockwise. Counterclockwise is the traditional route that trekkers take as it allows for better acclimatization; the Thorong La High Camp in this direction is at 4,900 meters (16,076 feet).

However, it means sharing much of the riding time and space with walkers. Although the cycling route doesn't strictly follow the exact trekking route, it is often still best for riders to just follow the road.

Riding clockwise avoids some of the traffic jams, with longer and more enjoyable descents—albeit at the risk of altitude-related illnesses. The final teahouse on the clockwise route is at 4,150 meters (13,616 feet) making for a 1,300-meter (4,265-foot) jump to the summit and far above the recommended 500-meter (1,640-foot) vertical maximum per day.

For those intent on doing the clockwise route, the key is to spend

SUMMITING THE THORONG LA PASS MEANS IT'S ALL DOWNHILL FROM HERE.

extra time between Muktinath and Manang. In the absence of a proper road here, hikers, porters, and horses must all share the same stretch of trail, making for much slower going.

"If I was to do the route again, I would do it in the counterclockwise direction, the same as the trekkers, to allow for better acclimatization," says Matty Waudby, who rode the route in 2018. "Altitude sickness is no joke. Either that or I'd spend more time acclimatizing in Muktinath. It was worth it though. The route really allowed me to realize how small we all are within Mother Nature and to focus on the things that matter the most." →

LOCALS CARRY SUPPLIES TO SUSTAIN THE MANY TOURIST-FOCUSED TEA HUTS.

NO TRIP TO NEPAL WOULD BE COMPLETE WITHOUT A KNITTED WOOL HAT.

For the most part, the terrain is not overly taxing. The vast majority of the route can be ridden (over 80 percent) and of that, much of it is a wide gravel jeep track. There are some sections of loose little rocks, as well as sharper gravel switchbacks where some off-road skills will be appreciated, but there is little to trouble most experienced cyclists. Despite this, a mountain bike is still the choice of most two-wheeled adventurers both for the range of gearing on offer as well as the extra comfort.

The greatest challenge of Annapurna is the altitude and lack of oxygen. Riders who have completed the circuit speak of breathlessly dragging bikes up the pass rather than struggling with the technicality of the terrain. With 10,000 meters (32,808 feet) of elevation over the route, the most common riding advice involves leaving as much excess gear as you can at home. ○

AWAY FROM THE TREKKING ROUTE COMES THE SERENITY YOU WOULD EXPECT OF THE HIGH MOUNTAINS.

ROUTE NOTES

Start and Finish: Pokhara, Nepal / **Distance:** 380 km (236 mi) / **Duration:** 1–2 weeks / **Category:** Multi-week circuit / **Terrain:** Rocky gravel, 75% off-road, 80 % rideable, 10,300 m (33,793 ft) of ascent / **Level:** Moderate, some off-road skills required

HIGHLIGHTS:

The circuit is roughly divided in two by the Thorong La pass, which is the crux of the route thanks to its 5,416 m (17,769 ft) peak. Going clockwise, the section between Muktinath and Manang is considered to be the most beautiful in the entire circuit.

LOCAL SPECIALTIES:

On the trail, trekkers, cyclists, and locals alike are powered by a regional staple called dal bhat: a base of boiled rice and stewed lentils.

WILDLIFE AND LANDSCAPE:

The circuit goes from 600 m (1,969 ft) above sea level, with hot and lush tropical forests, all the way up to the cold, windy, and virtually lifeless mountainsides well over 5,000 m (16,404 ft).

RESUPPLY NOTES:

Tea huts line the route and cater to Western tastes, although the local food is the real attraction. Try the *momo*: stuffed dumplings often served swimming in peppery tomato-based *jhol achar* sauce.

ACCOMMODATIONS:

The tea huts mean that shelter is never far away, and riders don't need to worry about carrying much in the way of overnight gear.

GETTING THERE (AND BACK):

Fly to Kathmandu. You can either cycle to Pokhara or arrange a private transfer.

RIDE SEASON:

April to May or October to November (peak seasons) are the best. Outside of this, weather can be unpredictable and monsoon-like.

EQUIPMENT:

Warm kit is needed for time off the bike, especially as overnight the temperatures can plummet well into the minus teens.

WHAT TO RIDE:

To maximize the enjoyment on the descents, a hardtail mountain bike would be the best choice.

OTHER IMPORTANT INFORMATION:

There are two permits required to ride the circuit: the Annapurna Conservation Area Permit (ACAP) and Trekkers' Information Management System (TIMS).

HISTORY:

Follows the well-worn trekking route, which has been in use since Nepal opened to tourism in the 1970s.

CONTRIBUTOR INFO:

Eileen Schwab is an experienced bikepacker from New Zealand. Matty Waudby is a well-traveled cycle tourer based in the U.K. They were joined by Emma Cornelis, Rob Hermans, Andy Hovey, and Clare Nattress.

MUKTINATH
Marshyangdi
MANANG
Annapurna
POKHARA
NEPAL
N

BMC

A CULTURAL FEAST IN RURAL SOUTHEAST ASIA

ROUTE:
HÀ GIANG LOOP

LOCATION:
VIETNAM

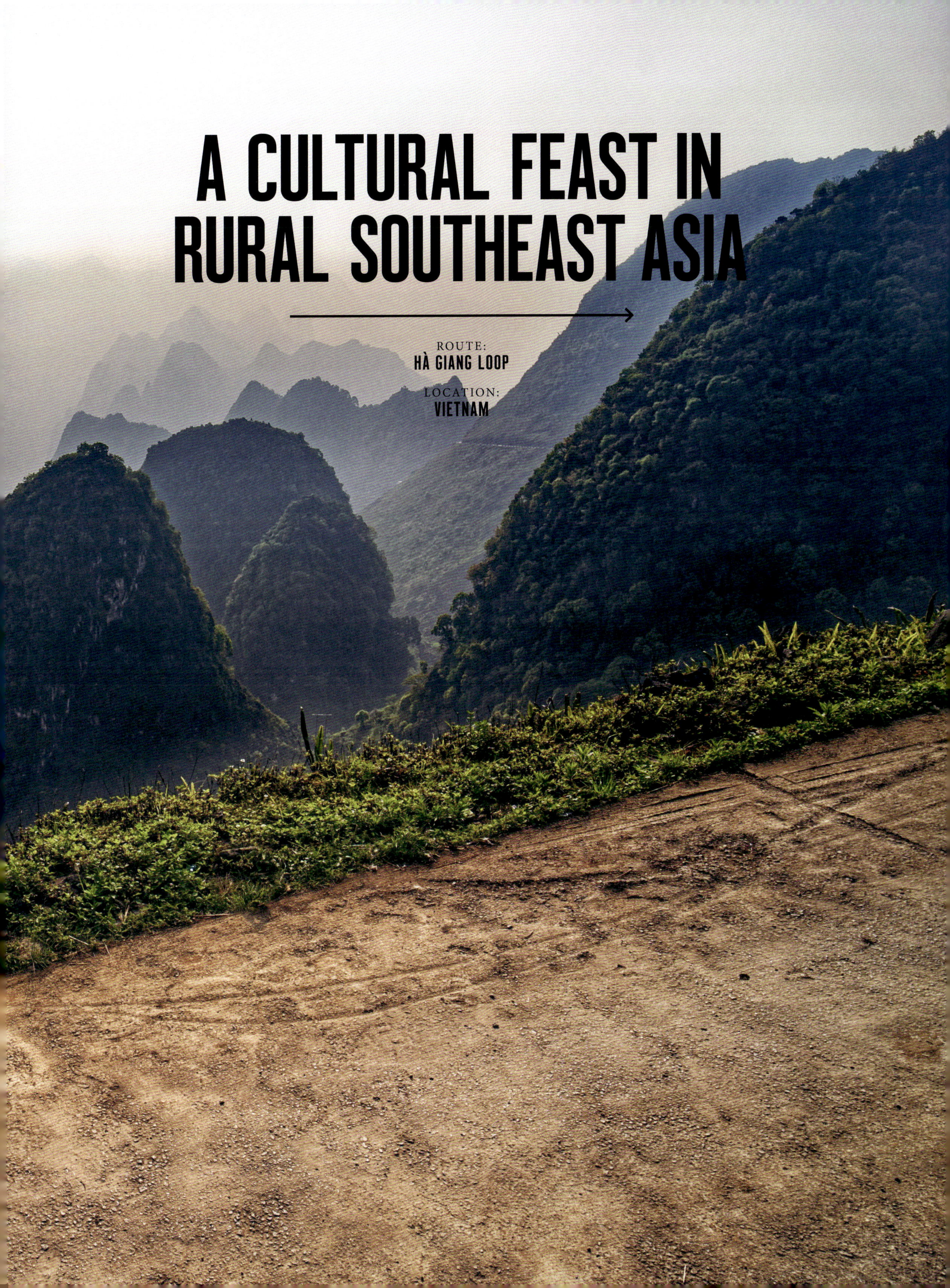

↑ THE RIVER CRUISE AT MEO VAC MAKES FOR A GOOD OFF-THE-BIKE DETOUR.
→ THE UNIQUE KARST PINNACLE SCENERY IS A MAJOR ATTRACTION OF THE HA GIANG LOOP.

IN NORTHERNMOST VIETNAM, on the country's frontier with China, lies the remote, rugged Hà Giang region. Vivid contours carve terraced fields into the mountains, while picturesque villages perch along narrow roads that weave like noodles around the famed karst pinnacles and valley floors. "Epic scenery, killer climbs, village life … what's not to like?" says Kenneth Koh. The Hà Giang Loop had long been on his bikepacking to-do list given its unofficial status as the most scenic route in Vietnam (perhaps in all of Southeast Asia). So, once the country was open for tourism post-pandemic, he and his wife, Laura, headed straight to Hanoi with their bikes in tow. "Everyone tends to go to the Sapa region, but a Vietnamese friend told us Hà Giang was a more genuine experience, especially for bikepacking," says Kenneth. "We plotted a seven-day route using the 'main' roads and passes on the official loop route while also seeking out some smaller backroads and trails."

As with many off-road bikepacking routes, intrepid motorcyclists share the roads and trails, with the same desire to head off the beaten track—just with different tools to do so. To that end, the Hà Giang Loop is actually much more established as a motorcycling route, but the light traffic and generally small roads—ranging from smooth tarmac to broken and loose dirt—make for an ideal cycling route too. The mountainous nature of the region and route, which packs in approximately 8,000 meters (26,000 feet) of climbing over 300 kilometers (186 miles), means the stunning riding comes with a caveat: such terrain commands a steadier daily average, typically 35–50 kilometers (22–31 miles), with 1,000–1,500 meters (3,000–5,000 feet) of climbing. Like the infamous morning mists that rise in the valleys, you'll be climbing through the day as temperatures soar. "Towns and villages are mostly at lower elevations in the plains close to a river, so there's usually a hill to climb as soon as you leave town," says Kenneth. "We kept the days short by hitting the hills in the cool of the early morning and rolling into villages before the heat of the afternoon peaked." Hà Giang's two highest peaks top out at about 2,400 meters (7,800 feet), with the main feature passes of the route—Mã Pí Lèng Pass (which links Đồng Văn and Mèo Vạc) and Quản Bạ Pass (known as Heaven's Gate)—climbing →

GIVEN THE HILLY TERRAIN AND CLIMATE, IT'S BEST TO SHIFT YOUR DAYS TO AVOID THE AFTERNOON HEAT.

"TOWNS AND VILLAGES ARE MOSTLY AT LOWER ELEVATIONS, THERE'S USUALLY A HILL TO CLIMB AS SOON AS YOU LEAVE TOWN."

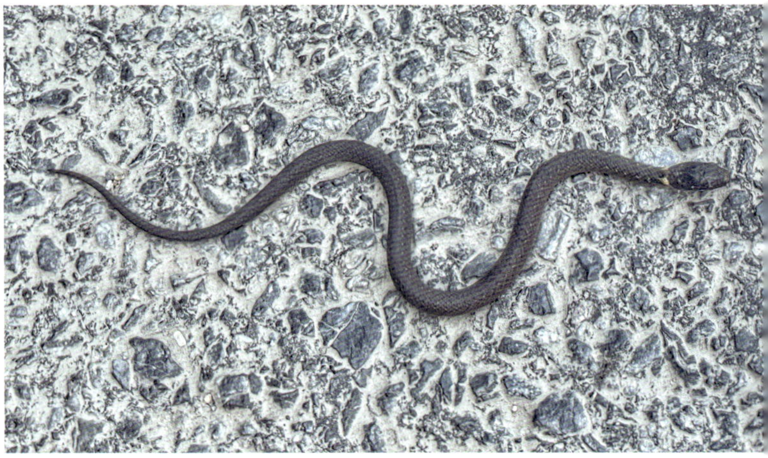

their way up to around 1,500 meters (5,000 feet). To help tick the meters off as you climb or descend, you'll notice roadside distance markers akin to the famous climbs of the European Alps and arterial routes through Asia.

Given the remoter, mountainous nature of Hà Giang, the population is still relatively low and ethnic Vietnamese. Expect to see peoples from Hmong, Tay, Yi, and Nùng backgrounds. In the villages, you'll be able to immerse yourself in Viet culture, be it food, farming, or at the bustling weekend markets, which represent a cacophony of peoples and cultures. Languages outside of Vietnam aren't heard regularly in these parts: "Hà Giang has less international tourism compared to some other countries in Southeast Asia; the infrastructure is mainly for domestic tourism," says Kenneth. "However, we found the Viet people to be friendly and helpful. Many times people would stop to help us order food or help with translation. It would be best to learn a few Viet phrases and words for the dishes you like, or if you have specific dietary needs, like vegetarian food, which isn't always a given." Agriculture is the main industry of the region, which is easy to see on the ride—rice, fruit, buckwheat, and, increasingly, tea—and no surprise, given the country was one of the first civilizations to practice agriculture due to its long coastline and lush terrain. Vietnam's location between the Indian and Pacific Oceans also meant it was one of the first melting pots for Indo-Chinese cultures, introducing Buddhism and Hinduism millennia ago.

To take a well-deserved break from the hilly riding, be sure to explore the villages on foot, and have a look into off-bike trips such as the river cruise at Mèo Vạc. Or, if enjoying Hà Giang by bike, look to add in detour sections like the Sky Path, a scenic concrete village doubletrack that becomes a twisty dirt singletrack as it rejoins the main QL4C road. You could even connect the main loop with the road heading south to Ba Bể Lake and Cao Bằng, for a bigger bikepacking trip. ○

SEEK OUT THE BUSTLING WEEKEND MARKETS IN TOWNS AND VILLAGES—A MELTING POT OF PEOPLES AND CULTURES.

ROUTE NOTES

Start and Finish: Ha Giang City, Vietnam / **Distance:** 300 km (186 mi) / **Duration:** 6–8 days / **Category:** Established touring route / **Terrain:** 90 % paved roads, 10 % gravel/singletrack, 8,000 m (26,247 ft) of ascent / **Level:** Moderate-Difficult

LOCAL SPECIALTIES:

All food is local Vietnamese, so there's not a lot of variety: *Pho* or rice noodles for breakfast, a *banh mi* (Vietnamese sandwich) for a mid-ride snack, *com tang* or fried rice for lunch, and usually rice with mixed dishes like spring rolls and tofu for dinner. Other regional dishes include *thang den*, *au tau porridge*, and *banh cuon* steamed rice rolls, often with egg. Vietnamese coffee packs a delicious, hearty punch and, as a digestivo, try the local rice wine—Vietnam's equivalent to whisky in Scotland.

WILDLIFE AND LANDSCAPE:

The route travels through karst peaks and valleys—limestone and granite that has eroded away to form distinctive outcrops above and below ground. Much of the loop lies within the Dong Van Karst Plateau Geopark, part of a series of UNESCO sites. Below, terraced, cultivated agricultural fields, livestock, and villages reign.

RESUPPLY NOTES:

It's worth stocking up on basics in Ha Giang but food, drink, and supplies are increasingly available in the many villages and towns along the route. It's easy to find local restaurants, and homestays will generally make you food.

ACCOMMODATIONS:

Given the terrain, there are very few places to camp, but accommodations can be found in the bigger centers along the route in the shape of guesthouses and homestays. In high season, accommodations are best booked in advance, even if the day before.

GETTING THERE (AND BACK):

Ha Giang is a small city and is the main gateway to the region. Somewhat remote and tucked away in northern Vietnam, it is around 300 km (186 mi) from Hanoi, the main center and transport hub. There are tourist buses/private minivans that run between Ha Giang and Hanoi—it takes around seven hours. You'll have to pay a little more for the bike, and you can store any bike boxes at your guesthouse.

RIDE SEASON:

There are two seasons: dry (September to May) and monsoon (May to September). The route can be ridden throughout most of the year, but ideally, avoid the super hot and wet monsoon season from June to August. The best time is probably January to April, which is relatively cool and dry. The hills and afternoon heat are the biggest challenges on a bicycle—plan to rise early to take advantage of the lower temperatures in the mornings.

EQUIPMENT:

Keep kit simple and light—camping or cooking gear isn't really needed, just layers to cope with the changing weather and conditions. It is worth carrying some food with you each day—maybe a *banh mi* Vietnamese sandwich, or two!

WHAT TO RIDE:

The route is technically all on established roads, but they are of varying conditions, so a gravel or bike with wider tires is best. Either way, bring a bike with a large cog and/or small chainring for grinding up the hills.

CONTRIBUTOR INFO:

A pilot in a previous life, Kenneth Koh has climbed Mount Everest, thru-hiked the Pacific Crest Trail, and was an adventure athlete for The North Face in Singapore for a decade. Together with his wife, Laura, he frequently heads off on bikepacking adventures. They rode the Ha Giang Loop in early 2022.

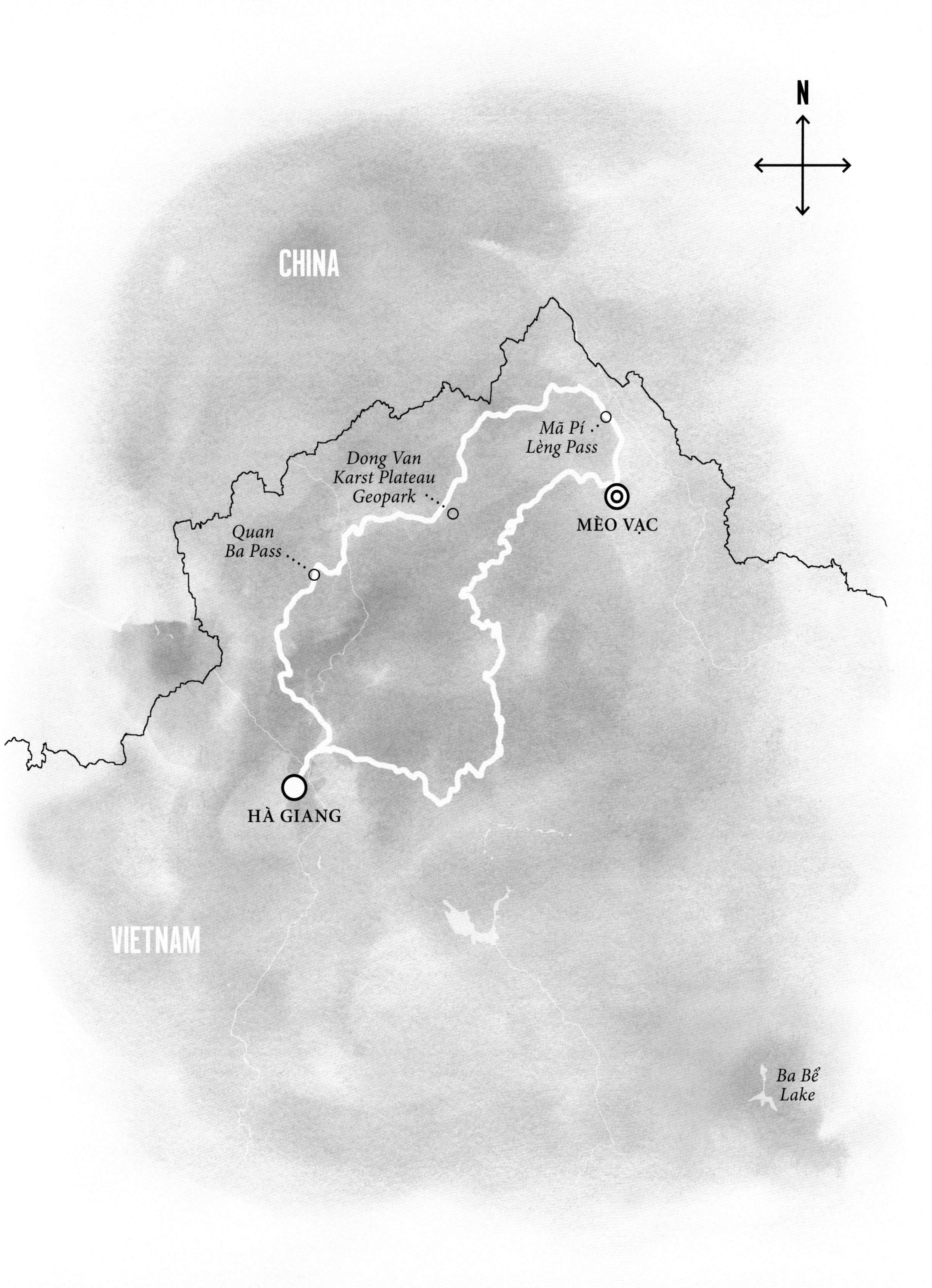
N
CHINA
Mã Pí
Lèng Pass
Dong Van
Karst Plateau
Geopark
Quan
Ba Pass
MÈO VẠC
HÀ GIANG
VIETNAM
Ba Bể
Lake

GETTING TO AND FROM YOUR ROUTE

No matter how long or arduous your chosen route, the journey to get there (and home again) can sometimes feel more challenging and exhausting than the pedaling. The second we aren't riding, the bicycle transforms from being an immensely practical and efficient tool for traveling into a bulky, awkward, and heavy encumbrance to smooth travel.

MAKING SUSTAINABLE DECISIONS
We all know the carbon impact of travel. Be mindful of how you can reduce your personal contribution. If it is possible to ride to the start, perfect. Taking the train is a low-impact alternative. If you need to drive, consider car-share options. If you are traveling overseas though, a plane is still the most practical mode of transport most of the time.

TRAINS
Depending on the country, trains can be an efficient and relaxed way of traveling with your bike—or deeply stressful, inconvenient, and even downright impossible. Research whether your chosen route allows bikes, and how much capacity there is on the train. It might be necessary to book your bike a place (sometimes for a small fee). In the worst-case scenario, you can deploy a few tricks. There are no rules about large bags on trains, so you can pack your bike into a flight case. We have even heard of people dismantling their bikes and wrapping them in heavy-duty trash bags to disguise their cargo.

PLANES
Airlines require bikes to be dismantled and transported in a protective case. There are lots of bags and boxes designed specifically for the job. The best will have wheels to make dragging it around the airport a little easier. Most have padding in the right places and do their utmost to stand up to the rigors of overzealous baggage handlers. Most airlines will require you to book this as "sporting goods" or similar and pay an extra fee. The weight limit for the bag normally allows you to stuff the cavities of the case with all of your bikepacking kit. Make sure you bring the right tools to rebuild your bike at the other end. Most airports have a left-luggage facility, where you can leave your empty bag for a daily fee. Alternatively, if you stay in a hotel before setting off, lots will be willing to store your bag while you are away if you ask nicely.

Remember that flying can be dehydrating. Drink plenty of water and stretch your legs regularly; your future self will thank you.

THROUGH ROUTES
Things get even more complicated if you are riding a point-to-point route and aren't planning to return to your starting point. If you are flying home from a different airport, you'll need to adjust your approach. To fly out, use the kind of large cardboard box that stores sell new bikes in. Your local store will happily put one aside for you if you give them a bit of notice. On the way home you have a few options:

- Call ahead to any local stores near the end of your ride, and ask if they can save you a box. They will usually do this for free, but it is good manners to make a purchase at the store in return.
- Some airports sell cardboard boxes for bikes but many don't.
- In the worst-case scenario, scavenge as much cardboard as you can from grocery stores etc., buy a few rolls of parcel tape, and get in touch with your crafting side.

Another consideration is travel clothing. You can, of course, fly in your riding kit. It might be more comfortable to wear some "burner" clothes on the way out and donate them to charity before you set off. You can then purchase some fresh threads at the end of your journey (or subject your fellow passengers to stinky lycra).

LAND OF THE LONG RIDE

ROUTE:
TOUR AOTEAROA

LOCATION:
NEW ZEALAND

↑ WHILST A ROUTE YOU CAN RIDE ANY TIME, THERE IS AN ANNUAL MASS-START BREVET OF THE TOUR AOTEAROA (TA), WHICH OVER 200 BIKEPACKERS RIDE, AND LOCAL COMMUNITIES REALLY GET BEHIND.
→ THE TA IS A NEW ZEALAND END-TO-END, ACROSS BOTH ISLANDS, THAT CONNECTS THE COUNTRY'S BEST OFF-ROAD RIDES, WITH THE MOST ENJOYABLE, LOGICAL BACK-COUNTRY ROADS.

AOTEAROA IS THE MĀORI NAME FOR NEW ZEALAND. Its closest translation is "land of the long white cloud," referring to the formations that regularly cling to its mountains. It is a fitting name for the Tour Aotearoa (TA), which winds its way beneath the clouds (and hopefully some sunshine) from the country's most northerly point to its most southerly, linking together the two large islands that form modern New Zealand.

In 2009, as a result of the global financial crisis, the New Zealand government started building cycle trails, to create jobs and establish a long-term national asset. Jonathan Kennett was a manager for the project, a job that entailed traveling the country inspecting the new trails as they were being constructed. As he did so, he realized it might be possible to link together the newly created Great Rides with the Heartland Rides to make a classic bikepacking route. It took another four years of research, but in 2016 the Tour Aotearoa was born, with 260 riders lining up at the first brevet.

Riders start at Cape Reinga, a location that Māori consider to be the most spiritually significant in the country. Known as "the leaping-off place of spirits," this is where the deceased make their way across the sea to the land of their ancestors. After staring out to sea from the lighthouse at the tip of the Cape, riders completing the TA turn landwards, with the whole country in front of them, beginning with a long stretch of sand known as Ninety Mile Beach. Māori names persist in New Zealand, especially on the North Island: the route passes through small and welcoming communities including Hukatere ("wind-driven sea-foam"), Ahipara ("sacred fire"), and Kohukohu (based on a curse uttered by the great Polynesian explorer Kupe when he was served undercooked food).

Perhaps the most spectacular section is the Timber Trail, which climbs through native forest to Mount Pureora at nearly 1,000 meters (3,280 feet) on 70 kilometers (43 miles) of singletrack and some sections of old logging road that crisscrosses river gorges via vertigo-inducing swing bridges.

Riders need to take the large ferry across the Cook Strait to the South Island, where the route follows a mix of paved roads, gravel roads, and rough 4 × 4 tracks over a high pass →

MAXXIS
ALPKIT
Energizer
COPPER KETTLE
Sea Salt
TWIX

TRAVERSING RURAL NEW ZEALAND MEANS CROSSING VARIOUS BODIES OF WATER ON FERRIES, SPEEDBOATS, STEAMSHIPS, AND FISHING BOATS.

"THOSE WHO COMPLETE THE ENTIRE RIDE FINISH IN ALMOST IDENTICAL STYLE TO HOW THEY START: STARING OUT ACROSS THE WAVES."

AFTER STARTING OUT AT SEA LEVEL ON A LONG, HARD-PACKED SAND BEACH SECTION IN THE NORTH, THE TA HEADS UP TO ITS 1,076-METER (3,530-FOOT) HIGH POINT IN THE CROWN RANGE, ON THE SOUTH ISLAND.

to Nelson. The 135-kilometer (84-mile) West Coast Wilderness Trail is often cited as a favorite; easy-going gravel along the coast that climbs its way into the hills. After reaching Queenstown—the tourist capital of NZ—a boat trip across Lake Wakatipu is followed by fantastic gravel-road riding to Southland. Then it is one long, but relatively easy, day of riding across the plains and down to Bluff, a small fishing town at the bottom of the South Island.

Those who complete the entire ride finish in almost identical style to how they start: staring out across the waves. Maybe a little wearier but with a whole country's worth of experiences under their belts. ○

ROUTE NOTES

Start: Cape Reinga, North Island, New Zealand / **Finish:** Bluff, South Island, New Zealand / **Distance:** 3,000 km (1,864 mi) / **Duration:** 10–30 days / **Category:** North-to-south epic journey / **Terrain:** 50–50 split between road and off-road / **Level:** Moderate

HIGHLIGHTS:

The sections of trail created by the New Zealand government make for great and varied riding. Waikato River Trail is already one of New Zealand's classic rides. The jet boat along Whanganui River is one of five boat trips on the tour, but definitely the most exhilarating.

LOCAL SPECIALTIES:

The Kiwi roast is a classic meal in New Zealand. It consists of roast beef/lamb and vegetables, with lavish amounts of gravy poured on top.

WILDLIFE AND LANDSCAPE:

The route passes Tāne Mahuta ("God of the Forest"), the largest known kauri tree standing today, in the Waipoua Forest. It is estimated to be between 1,250 and 2,500 years old.

RESUPPLY NOTES:

The ride is routed to allow for regular resupply in towns and villages along the entire distance.

ACCOMMODATIONS:

Many of the residential areas offer camping, hostel, or hotel accommodations. It is possible to complete the ride staying in accommodations each night.

GETTING THERE (AND BACK):

The nearest airport to the start is Auckland. The 130 km (80 mi) or so to the start is difficult to do via public transport—you may wish to book a shuttle.

RIDE SEASON:

The route is open all year round but best enjoyed in the late summer/early fall (Feb–April) of the Southern Hemisphere. Expect some rain but relatively mild temperatures.

EQUIPMENT:

No specific equipment is required. Some form of camp setup will allow for much more flexibility in terms of distances covered each day. You must wear a helmet by law while riding in New Zealand.

WHAT TO RIDE:

A gravel bike with high-volume tires or a lightweight mountain bike is most suitable. Some off-road sections are rough and rocky.

OTHER IMPORTANT INFORMATION:

The ride begins with a section along 90 Mile Beach, which is only passable around the hours of low tide. Check the tide timetables so that you know when to start your trip. There are several ferry crossings on the route and some have a limited number of crossings each day or week, so research crossing times.

ROUTEMAKER:

Jonathan Kennett, a New Zealand cyclist and cycling guidebook writer, created the route in 2016.

CONTRIBUTOR INFO:

Sven Martin is one of the most well known mountain bike photographers in the world. Tom Powell is a photographer based in Vancouver, Canada.

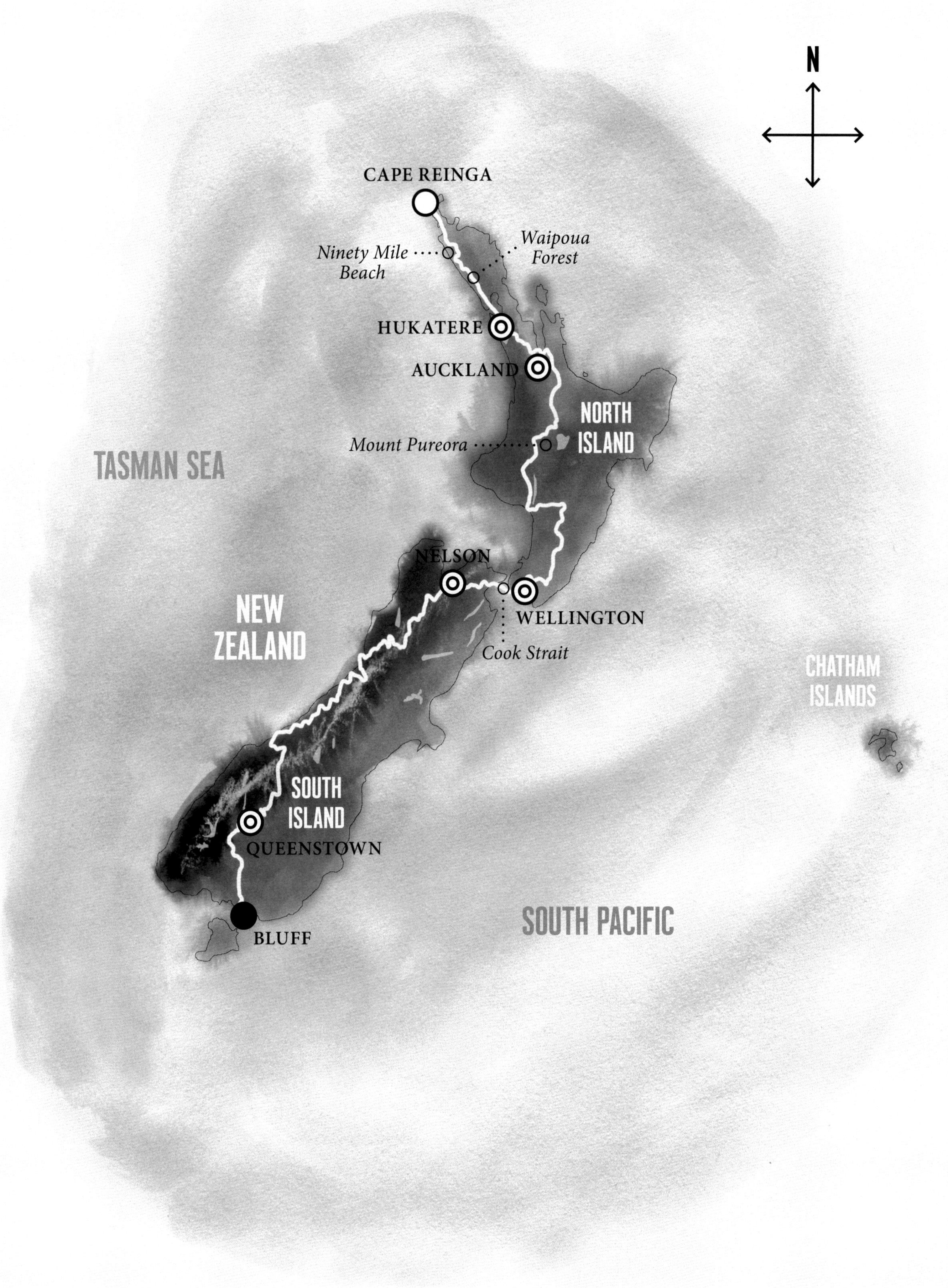

N
CAPE REINGA
Ninety Mile Beach
Waipoua Forest
HUKATERE
AUCKLAND
NORTH ISLAND
Mount Pureora
TASMAN SEA
NELSON
WELLINGTON
NEW ZEALAND
Cook Strait
CHATHAM ISLANDS
SOUTH ISLAND
QUEENSTOWN
SOUTH PACIFIC
BLUFF

THE ROOFTOP OF AUSTRALIA

ROUTE:
THE HUNT 1000

LOCATION:
AUSTRALIA

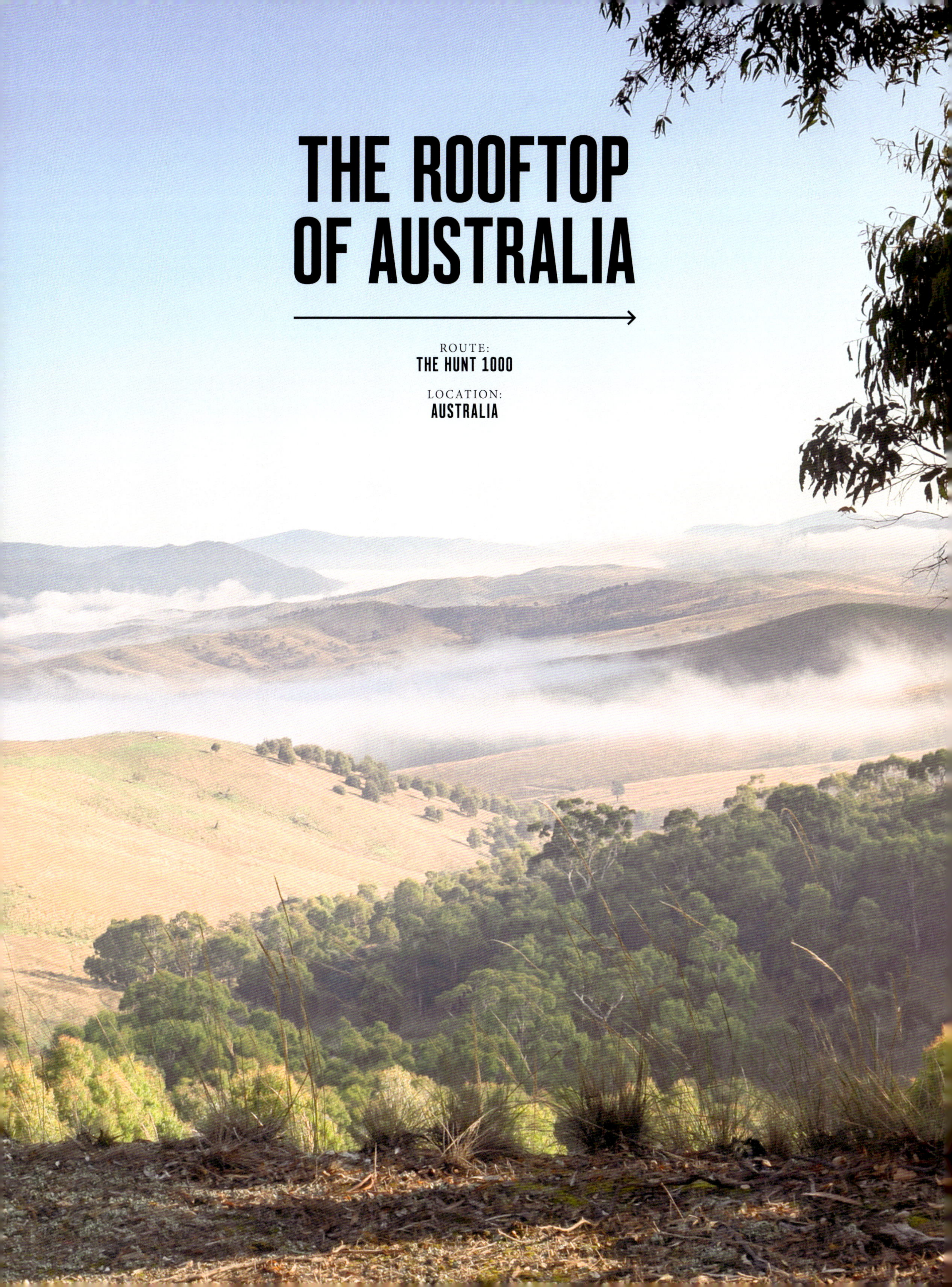

"MOSTLY OFF-ROAD, THE HUNT 1000 CATCHES THE EYE FOR THE REMOTENESS OF THE TERRAIN."

"I SAW MANY SNAKES out there on the trails, and I'm sure there were many more that I didn't see."

Not for the faint-hearted, the Hunt 1000. The route takes you on backcountry trails through the high country between Melbourne and Canberra in Australia's Capital Territory. High on the list in your bike luggage? As Matt Gould, a veteran of the route points out, a snake bandage is an absolute must given how much they enjoy warming themselves on the trail.

Even without the snakes, the Hunt 1000 enticed and intimidated Matt in equal measure for years before he eventually took the plunge, and it's not hard to understand why. The snakes are far from the only natural hazards on a route through the Australian Alps.

It was devised in 2016 by Australian bike builder Dan Hunt for the inaugural Hunt Bikes Snowy Mountains 1000 event. Dan had founded Hunt Bikes a year previously and decided the "1000" was the perfect terrain for their high-end bikepacking rigs.

Mostly off-road, it catches the eye for the remoteness of the terrain—and, somewhat surprisingly given Australia's sun, sea, and surf reputation, for the very real possibility of heavy snowfall and waist-high freezing river crossings. The route tops out at 1,800 meters (5,906 feet) and you'll need your climbing legs—there's nearly 20,000 meters (65,617 feet) of ascent across the 1,000-kilometer (621-mile) route.

Unless your name is Lachlan Morton, you'll need to carry camping equipment—there →

THE HUNT 1000 LINKS THE CITIES OF MELBOURNE AND CANBERRA, ACROSS THE AUSTRALIAN ALPS' ADVENTUROUS BACKCOUNTRY TRACKS AND TRAILS.

are sections in which there are 300 kilometers (186 miles) between towns. You'll also need to be happy to carry your bike at times, with some sections only negotiable on two feet (hike-a-bike) rather than two wheels.

In a 12-day riding of the route from Melbourne to Canberra, Dan spent the last four with no phone signal, no buddies (he didn't pass a single person), and no resupply points. This final section in the Jagungal Wilderness—depending on which way you choose to take it on—can often experience snowfall. Hunt 1000 riders down the years have had to shelter in emergency huts during snowfall or negotiate waist-high, freezing river crossings. The Jagungal Wilderness is in Kosciuszko National Park and is only accessible on bike or foot; it feels like something out of Jurassic Park, a remote wilderness that juxtaposes perfectly with the warm welcome you can expect when you do make it to the pockets of civilization en route.

The Australian Alps are 160 million years old and the nature of their formation means you'll be riding, once you've climbed up of course, on huge plateaus surrounded by vertiginous valleys. While in the mountains navigation is straightforward due to the lack of alternatives, making for a route that is simple yet uncompromising, much like the ubiquitous Australian staple you'll see at every pub stop en route: the chicken *parmi*. Australia's riff on a parmigiana, Australians will tell you they added the slice of ham under the cheese-topped chicken schnitzel to take it to another level. Americans will tell you it's their invention. Italians want nothing to do with it. Whatever its origins, it's likely you'll develop a love affair with the dish, as Matt explains: "It's an Aussie staple and something you'll find at every country pub. While nothing spectacular, it's a safe bet that the *parmi* will be the size of your plate and accompanied by a heavy serving of hot chips."

To the uninitiated, hot chips might be the last thing you'd expect to need on a long-distance Australian ride. But this is alpine territory—the route can only be ridden from spring to fall (October to March) because of snow and even in the height of summer, you should be prepared for snow in the high country. And if your ride coincides with heavy rain, it might end up being a little longer than 1,000 kilometers. There is a major river crossing—the Murray—on the New South Wales/Victoria border which can be impassable at times, meaning you'll have to detour around.

Make no mistake, the Hunt 1000 is a tough, and often lonely, route. If you don't like your own company, definitely take a friend or two. Whatever you do, take your strong legs—and an even stronger constitution. Those plate-sized chicken parmis take some digesting. ○

"THE HUNT 1000 IS A TOUGH, AND OFTEN LONELY, ROUTE. IF YOU DON'T LIKE YOUR OWN COMPANY, DEFINITELY TAKE A FRIEND OR TWO."

← A NETWORK OF BASIC ALPINE HUTS ARE DOTTED THROUGH THE WILDERNESS.
→ THE JAGUNGAL WILDERNESS AREA IS A CHALLENGING HIGHLIGHT.
↓ THIS REMOTE ROUTE CAN ONLY BE COMPLETED IN THE WARMER MONTHS BETWEEN OCTOBER AND MARCH.

ROUTE NOTES

Start: Melbourne, Victoria, Australia / **Finish:** Canberra, New South Wales, Australia (the route can be ridden in either direction) / **Distance:** 1,000 km/621 mi / **Duration:** 7–14 days / **Category:** Multi-week traverse / **Terrain:** 70 % off-road / **Level:** Moderate

LOCAL SPECIALTIES:

A plate-filling chicken *parmi* is one for the carnivores, but don't worry if you're vegetarian—the parmi is always served with hot chips and an optional plate of steamed vegetables.

WILDLIFE AND LANDSCAPE:

Seeing snakes is inevitable (carrying a snake bandage is essential) and you are also likely to spot a wild horse (aka a brumby) or two. The landscape is a mixture of high plains, even higher native forests, and snow gum woodlands.

RESUPPLY NOTES:

Beggars can't be choosers on the Hunt 1000. Resupply options are few and far between (with at least 100 km/62 mi between towns), so make the most of every single one. Water is less of a concern than food, given the proliferation of creeks and rivers on the route. The Hunt 1000 might be in the back of beyond, but it's not quite the Outback.

ACCOMMODATIONS:

There are pubs/motels on the route but, unless you're comfortable ticking off up to 300 km (186 mi) in a day, you're going to need to camp for at least half of your ride. Luckily, the campsites are some of Australia's best high country offerings—at the Licola Caravan Park, for example, you can have a post-ride swim in the Macalister River. It is worth remembering that in national parks, camping is only allowed in designated camping areas.

GETTING THERE (AND BACK):

Melbourne and Canberra are both major Australian cities, with international airports.

RIDE SEASON:

This ride needs to be completed from spring to fall (October to March) with snow making the route impassable outside of that time. On either side of that window you need to be prepared for freezing river crossings and potential blizzards. (In recent years, riders in November experienced blizzards.)

EQUIPMENT:

Other than the snake bandage, most of the gear required is standard for bikepacking. You must carry gear to deal with extreme weather conditions, even snowfall depending on the time of year. You'll also need to have the equipment and mechanical know-how to tackle any issues that arise with your bike. Pubs and bakeries are few and far between. Bike shops? Even rarer. Water is far from rare, but you'll need to have the means to treat it before drinking.

WHAT TO RIDE:

The ride is on fire trails, alpine paths, gravel tracks, and country roads. Route founder Dan Hunt recommends a mountain bike, advice Matt Gould was happy to follow (although he points out that you could complete it on a gravel bike). It is a technical route at times, so you'll need to be a decent bike handler. You'll also need to be able to handle carrying your rig as in some of the steeper, bumpier sections, hike-a-bike is the only option.

ROUTEMAKER:

Dan Hunt, the founder of Australian bike brand Hunt Bikes, designed the route in 2016.

CONTRIBUTOR INFO:

Matt Gould is a writer and photographer from Australia who focuses on the outdoor and adventure industry. He is the creator of Australian bikepacking journal Desire Lines CC. Matt is an experienced bikepacker, but taking on the Hunt 1000 was his longest, biggest, and most rewarding ride to date.

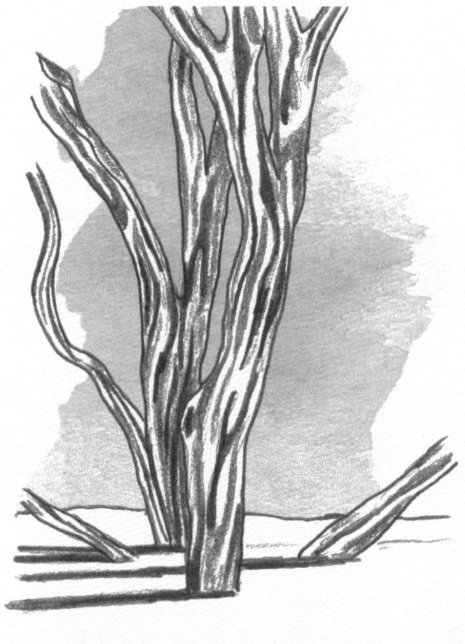

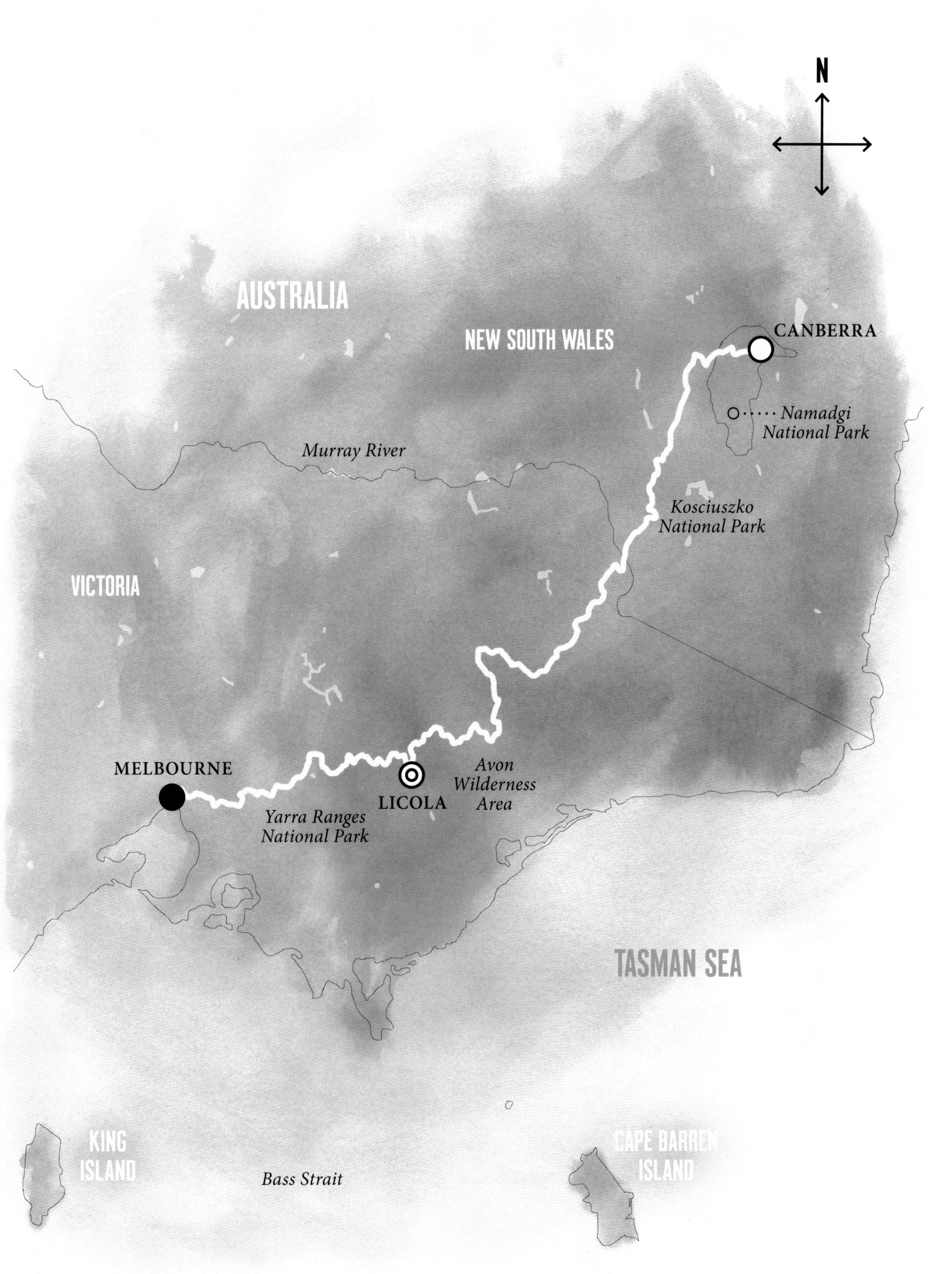
N
AUSTRALIA
NEW SOUTH WALES
CANBERRA
Namadgi National Park
Murray River
Kosciuszko National Park
VICTORIA
MELBOURNE
LICOLA
Avon Wilderness Area
Yarra Ranges National Park
TASMAN SEA
KING ISLAND
Bass Strait
CAPE BARREN ISLAND

INDEX

FOREWORD pp. 4–5
IMAGE: *Tom Gibbs*
instagram.com/bicycle_factory

TUSCANY TRAIL pp. 10–21
IMAGES: *Matteo Dunchi and Andrea Borchi (all images except for p. 13 top right), Matty Waudby (p. 13 top right)*
BIKEPACKERS: *Andrea Borchi*

TORINO-NICE RALLY pp. 22–31
IMAGES: *Tom Gibbs*
instagram.com/bicycle_factory

RAID PYRÉNÉES pp. 32–39
IMAGES: *Tom Hardie*
instagram.com/tomhardies

TOUR DU MONT BLANC pp. 40–49
IMAGES: *Trevor Worsey*
instagram.com/trevworsey

GR247 pp. 50–59
IMAGES: *Duncan Philpott (pp. 50–51, 53, 55), Stefan Rohner (pp. 52, 56, 57 bottom right), Katie-Jane L'Herpiniere (pp. 54, 57 top, 57 bottom left)*
duncanphilpott.com
instagram.com/duncanphilpott
stefan-rohner.net
katiejaneendurance.com
instagram.com/katiejaneendurance

GRANGUANCHE pp. 60–69
IMAGES: *Matteo Minelli (pp. 60–61, 62 bottom, 64–65, 66 top, 67 bottom), Alice Simpkins-Woods (pp. 62 top, 63 top, 63 bottom, 66 middle + bottom, 67 top)*
instagram.com/matminelli
granguanche.com
instagram.com/aliceswoods

ADRIATIC CREST pp. 70–83
IMAGES: *Ty Autrey (pp. 70–76, 77 top, 78 top + middle), Leslie Kehmeier (pp. 77 bottom, 78 bottom, 78/79 bottom, 79 top, 80–81)*
instagram.com/tys_view
thewideeyedworld.com
instagram.com/thewideeyedworld

TRANSCAUCASIAN TRAIL pp. 84–93
IMAGES: *Evan Christenson (pp. 84–88, 89 top, 90 top + bottom right), Chris Goodman (pp. 89 bottom, 90 bottom left, 91)*
evanchristenson.com
instagram.com/evanchristenson
uninspiredramblings.com
instagram.com/uninspiredramblings
ADDITIONAL CREDITS: *Tom Allen for founding the TCT organization, developing the route, and guiding the journey.*
transcaucasiantrail.com

CAIRNGORMS LOOP pp. 94–103
IMAGES: *Pannier.cc/Stefan Amato (p. 99), Pannier.cc/ Jordan Gibbons (pp. 94–97, 98, 100–101)*
pannier.cc
instagram.com/panniercc
jordangibbons.co.uk
instagram.com/gordanjibbons
BIKEPACKERS: *Stef Amato, Jordan Gibbons, and their friends Leonie and Harry*

SHELTER pp. 104–105
IMAGE: *Joffrey Maluski*
joffreymaluski.com
instagram.com/joffreymaluski

ICELAND DIVIDE pp. 106–119
IMAGES: *Joffrey Maluski*
joffreymaluski.com
instagram.com/joffreymaluski

TRAILSIDE FIXES pp. 120–121
IMAGE: *Michael Dammer*
instagram.com/el_taraumara

OREGON TIMBER TRAIL pp. 122–129
IMAGES: *Conan Thai*
conanthai.com
*instagram.com/everydaycult_*

COLORADO TRAIL pp. 130–137
IMAGES: *Michael Dammer*
instagram.com/el_taraumara

GREAT DIVIDE MOUNTAIN BIKE ROUTE pp. 138–147
IMAGES: *Spencer Harding*
spencerjharding.com
instagram.com/spencerjharding

COPING WITH EXTREMES pp. 148–149
IMAGES: *Joffrey Maluski (p. 148), Tom Gibbs (p. 149 top), Stan Engelbrecht (p. 149 bottom)*
joffreymaluski.com
instagram.com/joffreymaluski
instagram.com/bicycle_factory
instagram.com/stanengelbrecht

IDITAROD TRAIL pp. 150–161
IMAGES: *RJ Sauer*
instagram.com/rjsauer

PERU DIVIDE pp. 162–177
IMAGES: *Benjamin Johnson (pp. 162–165, 171 top), Martin Moreno Navarro (pp. 166–169, 170, 172–175)*
instagram.com/outsideandseek
instagram.com/nomadmartin

LA RUTA MALA pp. 178–187
IMAGES: *Mark Watson/Highluxphoto instagram.com/highluxphoto*
BIKEPACKERS: *Mark Watson, Hana Black*
ADDITIONAL CREDITS: *Route followed is published on bikepacking.com*

TRAVELING IN GROUPS pp. 188–189
IMAGES: *Stan Engelbrecht (p. 188), Chris Goodman (p. 189 top), Tom Gibbs (p. 189 bottom)*
instagram.com/stanengelbrecht
uninspiredramblings.com
instagram.com/uninspiredramblings
instagram.com/bicycle_factory

THE CROSS CAPE pp. 190–201
IMAGES: *Stan Engelbrecht (pp. 190–191, 194/195 below middle), Cape Cycle Routes (pp. 192–193, 194 top + bottom left, 195 top, 196–199)*
instagram.com/Stanengelbrecht
capecycleroutes.co.za

BARTANG VALLEY AND PAMIR HIGHWAY pp. 202–211
IMAGES: *Ryan Wilson (pp. 202–204, 205 bottom, 206–207, 208 top), Farawayistan/Robin Patijn and Sabina Knezevic (pp. 205 top, 208 bottom, 209)*
rmdub.com
instagram.com/rmdub
farawayistan.com
instagram.com/farawayistan

THE MIDDLE LANDS pp. 212–221
IMAGES: *Project Pedal Further/ Sara Bukies & Andreas Krucker (pp. 212–217, 218 bottom, 219 top), Mike Hayes (pp. 218 top, 219 bottom)*
projectpedalfurther.com
instagram.com/projectpedalfurther
seasurfdirt.com

TRAVELING IN REMOTE ENVIRONMENTS pp. 222–223
IMAGES: *Chris Goodman (p. 222), Leslie Kehmeier (p. 223 top), Farawayistan/Robin Patijn and Sabina Knezevic (p. 223 bottom)*
uninspiredramblings.com
instagram.com/uninspiredramblings
thewideeyedworld.com
instagram.com/thewideeyedworld
farawayistan.com
instagram.com/farawayistan

ANNAPURNA CIRCUIT pp. 224–235
IMAGES: *Eileen Schwab & Andy Hovey (pp. 224–225, 228, 231 bottom left, 232 top), Matty Waudby (pp. 226–227, 230), Farawayistan/Robin Patijn and Sabina Knezevic (pp. 229, 231 top left + right + bottom right, 232 bottom left + right, 233)*
instagram.com/eileenschwabnz
instagram.com/andyhovey
mattywaudby.com
instagram.com/getwildmatty
farawayistan.com
instagram.com/farawayistan

HA GIANG LOOP pp. 236–247
IMAGES: *Sam Rice & Bec Norman (pp. 240 top left, 242, 244 top left + right), Kenneth Koh (pp. 236–239, 240 top right + middle right + bottom right, 241, 243, 244 top, 245)*
instagram.com/adventurenomad
adventuresbycycle.com
instagram.com/adventuresbycycle

GETTING TO AND FROM YOUR ROUTE pp. 248–249
IMAGES: *Conan Thai (pp. 248, 249 bottom), Sven Martin (p. 249 top)*
conanthai.com
*instagram.com/everydaycult_*
instagram.com/svenmartinphoto

TOUR AOTEAROA pp. 250–261
IMAGES: *Tom Powell (pp. 250–251, 255 bottom, 256–259), Sven Martin (pp. 252–254, 255 top)*
tompowellphoto.com
instagram.com/tom_powell_photo
instagram.com/svenmartinphoto

THE HUNT 1000 pp. 262–269
IMAGES: *Mattie J Gould*
instagram.com/mattiejgould

GRAND BIKEPACKING JOURNEYS

Riding Iconic Routes around the World

This book was conceived, edited, and designed by gestalten.

Edited by Robert Klanten, Laura Allsop
Contributing editor: Stefan Amato

Foreword by Stefan Amato
Texts by Stefan Amato (pp. 6–9, 40–48, 94–105, 120–121, 236–246), Jordan Gibbons (pp. 162–186, 190–200, 212–220, 224–234), Tom Hill (pp. 22–38, 60–82, 106–118, 122–160, 188–189, 222–223, 248–260), and Tom Reynolds (pp. 10–20, 50–58, 84–92, 202–210, 262–268)

Illustrations by Stefan Amato (pp. 2, 6–9, 105, 121) and David Sparshott (pp. 20, 30, 38, 48, 58, 68, 82, 92, 102, 118, 128, 136, 146, 160, 176, 186, 200, 210, 220, 234, 246, 260, 268)

Map illustrations by Laetitia Hildebrand

Editorial Management by Lars Pietzschmann

Design by Isabelle Emmerich
Cover and layout by Melanie Ullrich

Photo Editors: Valentina Marinai, Madeline Dudley-Yates

Typefaces: *Montefiore* by The Entente, *Minion* Pro by Robert Slimbach

Cover image by Eileen Schwab and Andy Hovey
Back cover image by Duncan Philpott

Printed by Grafisches Centrum Cuno, Calbe (Saale)
Made in Germany

Published by gestalten, Berlin 2022
ISBN 978-3-96704-066-1

For more information, and to order books, please visit www.gestalten.com

Bibliographic information published by the Deutsche Nationalbibliothek. The Deutsche Nationalbibliothek lists this publication in the Deutsche Nationalbibliografie; detailed bibliographic data is available online at www.dnb.de

This book was printed on paper certified according to the standards of the FSC®.

FSC MIX Paper from responsible sources FSC® C043106